WONDER BOOK OF
MOTHER GOOSE

WONDER BOOK OF
MOTHER GOOSE

ILLUSTRATED BY FLORENCE CHOATE AND ELIZABETH CURTIS

DERRYDALE BOOKS

NEW YORK

This 2001 edition is published by Derrydale Books™,
an imprint of Random House Value Publishing, Inc.,
280 Park Avenue, New York, New York 10017.

Derrydale Books™ and design are trademarks of
Random House Value Publishing, Inc.

Random House
New York • Toronto • London • Sydney • Auckland
http://www.randomhouse.com/

Printed and bound in the United States of America

ISBN 0-517-16290-3

8 7 6 5 4 3 2 1

INDEX OF TITLES AND FIRST LINES

INDEX OF TITLES AND FIRST LINES

INDEX OF TITLES AND FIRST LINES

INDEX OF TITLES AND FIRST LINES

WONDER BOOK OF
MOTHER GOOSE

Old Mother Goose.

OLD MOTHER GOOSE, when
   She wanted to wander,
   Would ride through the air
On a very fine gander.

Mother Goose had a house,
'Twas built in a wood,
Where an owl at the door
For sentinel stood.

She had a son Jack,
A plain-looking lad,
He is not very good,
Nor yet very bad.

She sent him to market,
A live goose he bought,
"Here, mother," says he,
"It will not go for nought."

Jack's goose and her gander
Grew very fond;
They'd both eat together,
Or swim in one pond.

Jack found one morning,
As I have been told,
His goose had laid him
An egg of pure gold.

Jack ran to his mother,
The news for to tell,
She called him a good boy,
And said it was well.

[1]

Jack sold his gold egg
To a rogue named Lou,
Who cheated him out of
The half of his due.

Then Jack went a courting,
A lady so gay,
As fair as the lily,
And sweet as the May.

Then Lou and the Squire
Came behind his back,
And began to belabour
The sides of poor Jack.

Then old Mother Goose,
That instant came in,
And turned her son Jack
Into famed Harlequin.

She then with her wand,
Touched the lady so fine,
And turned her at once
Into sweet Columbine.

The gold egg into the sea
Was thrown then—
When Jack jumped in,
And got the egg back again.

Then Lou got the goose,
Which he vowed he would kill,
Resolving at once
His pockets to fill.

Jack's mother came in,
And caught the goose soon,
And mounting its back,
Flew up to the moon.

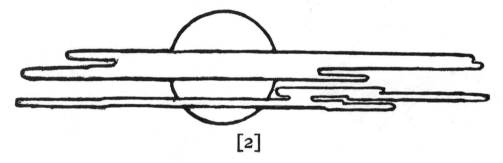

[2]

Fiddle, faddle, feedle.

THERE was an owl lived in an oak,
    Wisky, wasky, weedle;
    And every word he ever spoke
Was fiddle, faddle, feedle.

    A gunner chanced to come that way,
        Wisky, wasky, weedle;
        Says he, "I'll shoot you, silly bird,"
        Fiddle, faddle, feedle.

My Lady Wind.

MY lady Wind, my lady Wind,
    Went round about the house to find
    A chink to get her foot in:
She tried the key-hole in the door,
She tried the crevice in the floor,
    And drove the chimney soot in.

    And then one night when it was dark,
    She blew up such a tiny spark,
        That all the house was pothered:
    From it she raised up such a flame,
    As flamed away to Belting Lane,
        And White Cross folks were smothered.

        And thus when once, my little dears,
        A whisper reaches itching ears,
            The same will come, you'll find:
        Take my advice, restrain the tongue,
        Remember what old nurse has sung
            Of busy lady Wind!

[3]

Old Mother Hubbard.

OLD Mother Hubbard,
　　She went to the cupboard,
　　To give her poor dog a bone,
But when she came there
The cupboard was bare,
　　And so the poor dog had none.

She went to the baker's
　　To buy him some bread,
And when she came back
　　The poor dog was dead.

She went to the joiner's
　　To buy him a coffin,
And when she came back
　　The poor dog was laughing.

She took a clean dish
　　To get him some tripe,
And when she came back
He was smoking his pipe.

She went to the ale-house
　　To get him some beer,
And when she came back
　　The dog sat in a chair.

She went to the tavern
　　For white wine and red,
And when she came back
　　The dog stood on his head.

[4]

"OLD MOTHER HUBBARD, SHE WENT TO THE CUPBOARD"

She went to the hatter's
To buy him a hat,
And when she came back
He was feeding the cat.

She went to the barber's
To buy him a wig,
And when she came back
He was dancing a jig.

She went to the fruiterer's
To buy him some fruit,
And when she came back
He was playing the flute.

She went to the tailor's
To buy him a coat,
And when she came back
He was riding a goat.

She went to the cobbler's
To buy him some shoes,
And when she came back
He was reading the news.

She went to the sempstress
To buy him some linen,
And when she came back
The dog was spinning.

She went to the hosier's
To buy him some hose,
And when she came back
He was dressed in his clothes.

The dame made a curtsey,
The dog made a bow;
The dame said, "Your servant,"
The dog said, "Bow, wow!"

Little Miss Muffet.

LITTLE Miss Muffet sat on a tuffet,
Eating of curds and whey;
Along came a spider and sat down beside her,
And frightened Miss Muffet away.

[6]

When the Wind is in the East.

WHEN the wind is in the east,
    'Tis neither good for man nor beast;
    When the wind is in the north,
The skilful fisher goes not forth;
When the wind is in the south,
It blows the bait in the fishes' mouth;
When the wind is in the west,
Then 'tis at the very best.

John Cook.

JOHN COOK had a little grey mare; he, haw, hum!
    Her back stood up, and her bones they were bare; he, haw,
        hum!

John Cook was riding up Shuter's bank; he, haw, hum!
And there his nag did kick and prank; he, haw, hum!

John Cook was riding up Shuter's hill; he, haw, hum!
His mare fell down, and she made her will; he, haw, hum!

The bridle and saddle were laid on the shelf; he, haw, hum!
If you want any more you may sing it yourself; he, haw, hum!

Multiplication is Vexation.

MULTIPLICATION is vexation,
    Division is just as bad;
    The Rule of Three perplexes me,
And Practice drives me mad.

[7]

Six little Mice sat down to spin.

SIX little mice sat down to spin,
　　Pussy passed by, and she peeped in.
　　"What are you at, my little men?"
"Making coats for gentlemen."
"Shall I come in and bite off your thread?"
"No, no, Miss Pussy, you'll bite off our head."

Who killed Cock Robin?

WHO killed Cock Robin?
　　"I," said the sparrow,
　　"With my bow and arrow,
I killed Cock Robin."

Who saw him die?
　"I," said the fly,
　"With my little eye,
I saw him die."

Who caught his blood?
　"I," said the fish,
　"With my little dish,
I caught his blood."

[8]

Who'll make his shroud?
"I," said the beetle,
"With my thread and needle,
I'll make his shroud."

Who'll bear the torch?
"I," said the linnet,
"Will come in a minute,
I'll bear the torch."

Who'll be the clerk?
"I," said the lark,
"I'll say Amen in the dark,
I'll be the clerk."

Who'll dig his grave?
"I," said the owl,
"With my spade and shovel,
I'll dig his grave."

Who'll be the parson?
"I," said the rook,
"With my little book,
I'll be the parson."

Who'll be chief mourner?
"I," said the dove,
"I mourn for my love,
I'll be chief mourner."

Who'll sing his dirge?
"I," said the thrush,
"As I sing in a bush.
I'll sing his dirge."

Who'll carry his coffin?
"I," said the kite,
"If it be in the night,
I'll carry his coffin."

[9]

Who'll toll the bell?
  "I," said the bull,
  "Because I can pull,
I'll toll the bell."

All the birds of the air
  Fell sighing and sobbing,
When they heard the bell toll
  For poor Cock Robin.

God bless the Master of this House.

GOD bless the master of this house,
  The mistress bless also,
  And all the little children
That round the table go;
And all your kin and kinsmen,
  That dwell both far and near:
I wish you a merry Christmas,
  And a happy new year.

Tweedle-Dum and Tweedle-Dee.

TWEEDLE-DUM and Tweedle-dee
Resolved to have a battle,
For Tweedle-dum said Tweedle-dee
Had spoiled his nice new rattle.

Just then flew by a monstrous crow,
  As big as a tar barrel,
Which frightened both the heroes so,
  They quite forgot their quarrel.

[10]

The little Clock.

THERE'S a neat little clock,
    In the schoolroom it stands,
    And it points to the time
With its two little hands.

    And may we, like the clock,
        Keep a face clean and bright,
    With hands ever ready
        To do what is right.

In marble Walls.

IN marble walls as white as milk,
    Lined with a skin as soft as silk;
    Within a fountain crystal clear,
A golden apple doth appear.
No doors there are to this stronghold,
Yet thieves break in and steal the gold.
                                (An egg.)

The North Wind doth blow.

THE north wind doth blow,
    And we shall have snow,
    And what will poor Robin do then?
                Poor thing!

            He'll sit in a barn,
            And to keep himself warm,
        Will hide his head under his wing.
                                Poor thing!

[11]

Baa, baa, black Sheep.

BAA, baa, black sheep, have you any wool?
Yes, sir, yes, sir, three bags full:
One for the master, one for the dame,
And one for the little boy who lives in the lane.

So, merrily trip and go.

TRIP and go, heave and ho!
Up and down, to and fro;
From the town to the grove,
Two and two let us rove,
A-maying, a-playing;
Love hath no gainsaying!
So, merrily trip and go!
So, merrily trip and go!

As I was going to sell my Eggs.

AS I was going to sell my eggs
I met a man with bandy legs;
Bandy legs and crooked toes,
I tripped up his heels, and he fell on his nose.

Ride a Cock-Horse.

RIDE a Cock-Horse to Banbury Cross,
To see a fine lady on a white horse;
Rings on her fingers, and bells on her toes,
She shall have music wherever she goes.

[12]

"BAA, BAA, BLACK SHEEP, HAVE YOU ANY WOOL?"

Ride Away.

RIDE away, ride away, Johnny shall ride,
    And he shall have pussy-cat tied to one side;
    And he shall have little dog tied to the other;
And Johnny shall ride to see his grandmother.

An Apple Pie.

AN apple pie, when it looks nice,
    Would make one long to have a slice,
    But if the taste should prove so, too,
I fear one slice would scarcely do.
So to prevent my asking twice,
Pray, mamma, cut a good large slice.

Pitty Patty Polt.

PITTY Patty Polt,
    Shoe the wild colt!
    Here a nail, and there a nail,
Pitty Patty Polt.

I had a little Nut Tree.

I HAD a little nut tree, nothing would it bear
    But a silver apple and a golden pear;
    The King of Spain's daughter came to see me,
And all for the sake of my little nut tree.
I skipped over water, I danced over sea,
And all the birds in the air couldn't catch me.

A Puzzle.

HAVE you seen the old woman of Banbury Cross,
Who rode to the fair on the top of her horse?
And since her return she still tells, up and down,
Of the wonderful lady she saw when in town.
She has a small mirror in each of her eyes,
And her nose is a bellows of minnikin size;
There's a neat little drum fix'd in each of her ears,
Which beats a tattoo to whatever she hears.
She has in each jaw a fine ivory mill,
And day after day she keeps grinding it still.
Both an organ and flute in her small throat are placed,
And they are played by a steam engine worked in her breast.
But the wonder of all, in her mouth it is said,
She keeps a loud bell that might waken the dead;
And so frightened the woman, and startled the horse,
That they galloped full speed back to Banbury Cross.

Fire, Fire.

FIRE! fire!" said the town crier;
"Where? where?" said Goody Blair;
"Down the town," said Goody Brown;
"I'll go and see 't," said Goody Fleet;
"So will I," said Goody Fry.

Rock-a-bye, Baby.

ROCK-A-BYE, baby, thy cradle is green;
Father's a nobleman, mother's a queen;
And Betty's a lady, and wears a gold ring;
And Johnny's a drummer, and drums for the king.

[15]

Hush-a-bye, Baby.

HUSH-A-BYE, baby, on the tree top,
   When the wind blows, the cradle will rock;
   When the bough bends the cradle will fall,
Down will come baby, bough, cradle, and all.

Birds, Beasts, and Fishes.

THE Dog will come when he is called,
   The Cat will walk away;
   The Monkey's cheek is very bald;
  The Goat is fond of play.
The Parrot is a prate-apace,
  Yet knows not what he says:
The noble Horse will win the race,
  Or draw you in a chaise.

        The Pig is not a feeder nice,
          The Squirrel loves a nut,
        The Wolf would eat you in a trice,
          The Buzzard's eyes are shut.
        The Lark sings high up in the air,
          The Linnet in the tree;
        The Swan he has a bosom fair,
          And who so proud as he?

Oh, yes, the Peacock is more proud,
  Because his tail has eyes;
The Lion roars so very loud,
  He'd fill you with surprise.
The Raven's coat is shining black,
  Or, rather, raven-grey:
The Camel's bunch is on his back,
  The Owl abhors the day.

The Sparrow steals the cherry ripe,
　　The Elephant is wise,
The Blackbird charms you with his pipe,
　　The false Hyena cries.
The Hen guards well her little chicks,
　　The Cow—her hoof is slit:
The Beaver builds with mud and sticks,
　　The Lapwing cries "Peewit."

The little Wren is very small,
　　The Humming-bird is less;
The Lady-bird is least of all,
　　And beautiful in dress.
The Pelican she loves her young,
　　The Stork its parent loves;
The Woodcock's bill is very long,
　　And innocent are Doves.

The streaked Tiger's fond of blood,
　　The Pigeon feeds on peas,
The Duck will gobble in the mud,
　　The Mice will eat your cheese.
A Lobster's black, when boiled he's red,
　　The harmless Lamb must bleed;
The Cod-fish has a clumsy head,
　　The Goose on grass will feed.

[17]

The lady in her gown of silk,
  The little Worm may thank;
The sick man drinks the Ass's milk,
  The Weasel's long and lank.
The Buck gives us a venison dish,
  When hunted for the spoil:
The Shark eats up the little fish,
  The Whale produces oil.

The Glow-worm shines the darkest night,
  With Lantern in his tail;
The Turtle is the cit's delight,
  And wears a coat of mail.
In Germany they hunt the Boar,
  The Bee brings honey home,
The Ant lays up a winter store,
  The Bear loves honey-comb.

The Eagle has a crooked beak,
  The Plaice has orange spots;
The Starling, if he's taught, will speak;
  The Ostrich walks and trots.
The child that does not these things know,
  Might well be called a dunce;
But I in knowledge quick will grow,
  For youth can come but once.

Jack and Jill.

JACK and Jill went up the hill,
  To fetch a pail of water;
Jack fell down and broke his crown,
  And Jill came tumbling after.

"JACK AND JILL WENT UP THE HILL"

History of John Gilpin.

JOHN GILPIN was a citizen
  Of credit and renown,
  A train-band captain eke was he,
  Of famous London town.

  John Gilpin's spouse said to her dear,
    "Though wedded we have been
  These twice ten tedious years, yet we
    No holiday have seen.

    "To-morrow is our wedding-day,
      And we will then repair
    Unto the 'Bell' at Edmonton,
      All in a chaise and pair.

"My sister, and my sister's child,
  Myself, and children three,
Will fill the chaise; so you must ride
  On horseback after we."

    He soon replied, "I do admire
      Of womankind but one,
    And you are she, my dearest dear,
      Therefore it shall be done.

    "I am a linendraper bold,
      As all the world doth know,
    And my good friend the calender
      Will lend his horse to go."

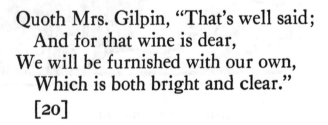

      Quoth Mrs. Gilpin, "That's well said;
        And for that wine is dear,
      We will be furnished with our own,
        Which is both bright and clear."

[20]

John Gilpin kissed his loving wife;
　O'erjoyed was he to find,
That though on pleasure she was bent,
　She had a frugal mind.

The morning came, the chaise was brought,
　But yet was not allowed
To drive up to the door, lest all
　Should say that she was proud.

So three doors off the chaise was stayed,
　Where they did all get in;
Six precious souls, and all agog
　To dash through thick and thin.

Smack went the whip, round went the wheels,
　Were never folks so glad!
The stones did rattle underneath,
　As if Cheapside were mad.

John Gilpin at his horse's side
　Seized fast the flowing mane,
And up he got, in haste to ride,
　But soon came down again.

For saddletree scarce reached had he,
　His journey to begin,
When, turning round his head, he saw
　Three customers come in.

So down he came; for loss of time,
　Although it grieved him sore,
Yet loss of pence, full well he knew,
　Would trouble him much more.

'Twas long before the customers
　Were suited to their mind,
When Betty screaming came downstairs,
　"The wine is left behind!"

[21]

"Good lack!" quoth he, "yet bring it me,
My leathern belt likewise,
In which I bear my trusty sword
When I do exercise."

Now Mistress Gilpin (careful soul!)
Had two stone bottles found,
To hold the liquor that she loved,
And keep it safe and sound.

Each bottle had a curling ear,
Through which the belt he drew,
And hung a bottle on each side,
To make his balance true.

Then over all, that he might be
Equipped from top to toe,
His long red cloak, well brushed and neat,
He manfully did throw.

Now see him mounted once again
Upon his nimble steed,
Full slowly pacing o'er the stones,
With caution and good heed.

But finding soon a smoother road
Beneath his well-shod feet,
The snorting beast began to trot,
Which galled him in his seat.

"So, fair and softly!" John he cried,
But John he cried in vain;
That trot became a gallop soon,
In spite of curb and rein.

So stooping down, as needs he must
Who cannot sit upright,
He grasped the mane with both his hands,
And eke with all his might.

[22]

His horse, who never in that sort
  Had handled been before,
What thing upon his back had got,
  Did wonder more and more.

    Away went Gilpin, neck or nought;
      Away went hat and wig;
    He little dreamt, when he set out,
      Of running such a rig.

        The wind did blow, the cloak did fly
          Like streamer long and gay,
        Till, loop and button failing both,
          At last it flew away.

           Then might all people well discern
             The bottles he had slung;
           A bottle swinging at each side,
             As hath been said or sung.

The dogs did bark, the children screamed,
  Up flew the windows all;
And every soul cried out, "Well done!"
  As loud as he could bawl.

    Away went Gilpin—who but he?
      His fame soon spread around:
    "He carries weight! he rides a race!
    'Tis for a thousand pound!"

        And still as fast as he drew near,
          'Twas wonderful to view
        How in a trice the turnpike-men
          Their gates wide open threw.

           And now, as he went bowing down
             His reeking head full low,
           The bottles twain behind his back
             Were shattered at a blow.

Down ran the wine into the road,
  Most piteous to be seen,
Which made the horse's flanks to smoke
  As they had basted been.

    But still he seemed to carry weight,
      With leathern girdle braced;
    For all might see the bottle-necks
      Still dangling at his waist.

        Thus all through merry Islington
          These gambols he did play,
        Until he came unto the Wash
          Of Edmonton so gay;

            And there he threw the wash about
              On both sides of the way,
            Just like unto a trundling mop,
              Or a wild goose at play.

At Edmonton his loving wife
  From the balcony spied
Her tender husband, wondering much
  To see how he did ride.

    "Stop, stop, John Gilpin!—Here's the house!"
      They all at once did cry;
    "The dinner waits, and we are tired."
      Said Gilpin—"So am I!"

        But yet his horse was not a whit
          Inclined to tarry there;
        For why?—his owner had a house
          Full ten miles off, at Ware.

            So like an arrow swift he flew,
              Shot by an archer strong;
            So did he fly—which brings me to
              The middle of my song.

[24]

Away went Gilpin out of breath
And sore against his will,
Till at his friend the calender's,
His horse at last stood still.

The calender, amazed to see
His neighbour in such trim,
Laid down his pipe, flew to the gate,
And thus accosted him:

"What news? what news? your tidings tell;
Tell me you must and shall—
Say why bareheaded you are come,
Or why you come at all?"

Now Gilpin had a pleasant wit,
And loved a timely joke;
And thus unto the calender
In merry guise he spoke:

"I came because your horse would come:
And, if I well forebode,
My hat and wig will soon be here,
They are upon the road."

The calender, right glad to find
His friend in merry pin,
Returned him not a single word,
But to the house went in;

Whence straight he came with hat and wig,
A wig that flowed behind,
A hat not much the worse for wear,
Each comely in its kind.

He held them up, and in his turn
Thus showed his ready wit,
"My head is twice as big as yours,
They therefore needs must fit.

[25]

"But let me scrape the dirt away,
  That hangs upon your face;
And stop and eat, for well you may
  Be in a hungry case."

Said John, "It is my wedding-day,
  And all the world would stare
If wife should dine at Edmonton,
  And I should dine at Ware."

So turning to his horse, he said,
  "I am in haste to dine;
'Twas for your pleasure you came here,
  You shall go back for mine."

Ah! luckless speech, and bootless boast!
  For which he paid full dear;
For while he spake, a braying ass
  Did sing most loud and clear;

Whereat his horse did snort, as he
  Had heard a lion roar,
And galloped off with all his might,
  As he had done before.

Away went Gilpin, and away
  Went Gilpin's hat and wig:
He lost them sooner than at first,
  For why—they were too big.

Now Mistress Gilpin, when she saw
  Her husband posting down
Into the country far away,
  She pulled out half-a-crown;

And thus unto the youth she said,
  That drove them to the "Bell,"
"This shall be yours when you bring back
  My husband safe and well."

[26]

The youth did ride, and soon did meet
  John coming back amain;
Whom in a trice he tried to stop,
  By catching at his rein;

    But not performing what he meant,
      And gladly would have done,
    The frightened steed he frighted more,
      And made him faster run.

      Away went Gilpin, and away
        Went postboy at his heels,
      The postboy's horse right glad to miss
        The lumbering of the wheels.

        Six gentlemen upon the road,
          Thus seeing Gilpin fly,
        With postboy scampering in the rear,
          They raised the hue and cry.

"Stop thief! stop thief! a highwayman!"
  Not one of them was mute;
And all and each that passed that way
  Did join in the pursuit.

    And now the turnpike gates again
      Flew open in short space;
    The toll-men thinking, as before,
      That Gilpin rode a race.

      And so he did, and won it too,
        For he got first to town;
      Nor stopped till where he had got up,
        He did again get down.

        Now let us sing, "Long live the King,
          And Gilpin, long live he;"
        And when he next doth ride abroad,
          May I be there to see.

Peter Piper.

PETER PIPER picked a peck of pickled pepper;
A peck of pickled pepper Peter Piper picked;
If Peter Piper picked a peck of pickled pepper,
Where's the peck of pickled pepper Peter Piper picked?

London Bridge is falling down.

LONDON Bridge is falling down,
Falling down, falling down;
London Bridge is falling down,
My fair lady.

You've stole my watch and kept my keys,
Kept my keys, kept my keys;
You've stole my watch and kept my keys,
My fair lady.

Off to prison she must go,
She must go, she must go;
Off to prison she must go,
My fair lady.

Take the key and lock her up,
Lock her up, lock her up;
Take the key and lock her up,
My fair lady.

Bryan O'Lin.

BRYAN O'LIN had no breeches to wear
So he bought him a sheepskin and made him a pair.

With the skinny side out, and the woolly side in,
"Ah ha, that is warm!" said Bryan O'Lin.

"We are three Brethren out of Spain."

WE are three brethren out of Spain,
Come to court your daughter Jane."
"My daughter Jane she is too young,
She has not learned her mother tongue."

"Be she young, or be she old,
For her beauty she must be sold.
So fare you well, my lady gay,
We'll call again another day."

"Turn back, turn back, thou scornful knight,
And rub thy spurs till they be bright."
"Of my spurs take you no thought,
For in this land they were not bought.
So fare you well, my lady gay,
We'll call again another day."

"Turn back, turn back, thou scornful knight;
And take the fairest in your sight."
"The fairest maid that I can see,
Is pretty Nancy, come to me."

"Here comes your daughter, safe and sound,
Every pocket with a thousand pound,
Every pocket with a gay gold ring,
Please to take your daughter in."

The Girl in the Lane, that couldn't speak Plain.

THE girl in the lane, that couldn't speak plain,
Cried, gobble, gobble, gobble:
The man on the hill, that couldn't stand still,
Went hobble, hobble, hobble.

[29]

A Farmer went trotting upon his grey Mare.

A FARMER went trotting upon his grey mare,
    Bumpety, bumpety, bump!
With his daughter behind him so rosy and fair,
    Lumpety, lumpety, lump!

A raven cried "Croak!" and they all tumbled down,
    Bumpety, bumpety, bump!
The mare broke her knees, and the farmer his crown,
    Lumpety, lumpety, lump!

The mischievous raven flew laughing away,
    Bumpety, bumpety, bump!
And vowed he would serve them the same the next day,
    Lumpety, lumpety, lump!

Tom, Tom, the Piper's Son.

TOM, Tom, the piper's son,
    Stole a pig, and away he run;
    The pig was eat and Tom was beat,
And Tom ran crying down the street.

Little Tom Twig.

LITTLE Tom Twig bought a fine bow and arrow,
    And what did he shoot? why, a poor little sparrow,
    Oh, fie, little Tom, with your fine bow and arrow.
How cruel to shoot at a poor little sparrow.

"TOM, TOM, THE PIPER'S SON, STOLE A PIG, AND AWAY HE RUN"

Elsie Marley.

ELSIE MARLEY is grown so fine,
　　She won't get up to serve the swine,
　　But lies in bed till eight or nine,
And surely she does take her time.

　　　　And do you ken Elsie Marley, honey?
　　　　The wife who sells the barley, honey;
　　　　She won't get up to serve her swine,
　　　　And do you ken Elise Marley, honey?

Two little Dogs.

TWO little dogs
　　Sat by the fire,
　　Over a fender of coal-dust;
Said one little dog
To the other little dog,
If you don't talk, why, I must.

Hey, diddle, diddle.

HEY, diddle, diddle!
　　The cat and the fiddle;
　　The cow jumped over the moon.
The little dog laughed
To see such craft;
And the dish ran away with the spoon.

[32]

There was a Monkey.

THERE was a monkey climb'd up a tree,
When he fell down, then down fell he.

There was a crow sat on a stone,
When he was gone, then there was none.

There was an old wife did eat an apple,
When she had ate two, she had ate a couple.

There was a horse going to the mill,
When he went on, he stood not still.

There was a butcher cut his thumb,
When it did bleed, then blood did come.

There was a lackey ran a race,
When he ran fast, he ran apace.

There was a cobbler clowting shoon,
When they were mended, they were done.

There was a chandler making candle,
When he them strip, he did them handle.

There was a navy went into Spain,
When it return'd, it came again.

Little King Boggen.

LITTLE King Boggen he built a fine hall,
Pie-crust and pastry-crust, that was the wall;
The windows were made of black-puddings and white,
And slated with pancakes;—you ne'er saw the like.

The Champions of Christendom.

IN Egypt was a dragon dire
  With scales of steel, and breath of fire:
  And Egypt's Princess fair and good
Was doomed to be the monster's food:
St. George this fearful dragon slew,
And for his wife gained Sebra true.

St. Andrew, Scotland's famous knight,
In deeds of valour took delight;
Maidens in grief and matrons grave
From insult he was wont to save.
For noble deeds he was renowned:
His fame did through the world resound.

St. Andrew fought, as we are told,
Against a host of warriors bold:
They viewed his strength with wonderment,
And yielding, in submission bent.
Defeated by his powerful rod,
They owned the greatness of his GOD.

St. David, Welshman's Champion bold,
Preferred rude war to ease and gold:
He, fighting for his faith divine,
Unhorsed and slew Prince Palestine.
His Pagan followers stood in awe,
And worshipped heathen gods no more.

[34]

St. Patrick, Ireland's valiant knight,
Did thirty robbers put to flight;
Rescued from them six ladies fair,
And then protected them with care.
Great fame and glory he acquired,
And as a holy priest expired.

St. Dennis was the knight of France,
As brave as ever carried lance:
Fair fame he won: for he did free
A princess prisoned in a tree.
Fair Eglantine, once Thessaly's pride,
He saved and took to be his bride.

St. James the Champion was of Spain,
His country's glory to maintain:
An angry boar, inflamed with rage,
This hero did in fight engage.
And since he slew the boar in strife,
He Celestine did gain as wife.

St. Anthony, Italian knight,
His country's fame upheld in fight:
The giant Blanderon did place
In prison dark the Queen of Thrace;
St. Anthony the giant slew
And took as wife the princess true.

Daffy-down-dilly.

DAFFY-DOWN-DILLY is new come to town,
With a petticoat green and a bright yellow gown.

[35]

I have been to Market.

I HAVE been to market, my lady, my lady.
  Then you've not been to the fair, says pussy, says pussy.
  I bought me a rabbit, my lady, my lady.
Then you did not buy a hare, says pussy, says pussy.

As white as Milk.

AS white as milk,
    And not milk;
    As green as grass,
And not grass;
As red as blood,
And not blood;
As black as soot,
And not soot!

(*A bramble blossom.*)

One to make ready.

ONE to make ready,
    And two to prepare;
    Good luck to the rider,
And away goes the mare.

Ride a Cock-horse to Banbury Cross.

RIDE a cock-horse to Banbury Cross
    To see what Tommy can buy;
    A penny white loaf, a penny white cake,
And a two-penny apple pie.

[36]

"RIDE A COCK-HORSE TO BANBURY CROSS"

Little Boy Blue.

LITTLE Boy Blue, go blow your horn,
The sheep's in the meadow, the cow's in the corn.
Where's the little boy, that tends the sheep?
He's under the haycock fast asleep.

As I was going to St. Ives.

AS I was going to St. Ives
I met a man with seven wives;
Each wife had seven sacks,
In each sack were seven cats,
And each cat had seven kits.
Kits, cats, sacks, and wives,
How many were going to St. Ives?

Intery, mintery, cutery-corn.

INTERY, mintery, cutery-corn,
Apple seed and apple thorn;
Wine, brier, limber-lock,
Five geese in a flock,
Sit and sing by a spring,
O-u-t, and in again.

Barber, Barber.

BARBER, barber, shave a pig,
How many hairs will make a wig?
"Four and twenty, that's enough."
Give the barber a pinch of snuff.

Bow, wow, says the Dog.

BOW, wow, says the dog;
    Mew, mew, says the cat;
    Grunt, grunt, goes the hog;
And squeak goes the rat.

    Chirp, chirp, says the sparrow;
      Caw, caw, says the crow;
    Quack, quack, says the duck;
      And what cuckoos say, you know.

      So, with sparrows and cuckoos;
        With rats and with dogs;
      With ducks and with crows;
        With cats and with hogs;

        A fine song I have made,
          To please you, my dear;
        And if it's well sung,
          'Twill be charming to hear.

Billy Pringle's Pig.

HAVE you ever heard of Billy Pringle's pig?
    It was very little and not very big;
    When it was alive it lived in clover;
But now it's dead, and that's all over.
Billy Pringle he lay down and died,
Betsey Pringle she sat down and cried;
So there's an end of all the three,
Billy Pringle he, Betsy Pringle she, and poor little piggy wigee.

The Babes in the Wood.

A GENTLEMAN of good account
   In Norfolk dwelt of late,
Whose wealth and riches did surmount
Most men of his estate.

Sore sick he was, and like to die,
   No help his life could save;
His wife by him as sick did lie,
   And both were near the grave.

No love between these two was lost:
   Each to the other kind;
In love they lived, in love they died,
   And left two babes behind.

Now, if the children chanced to die,
   Ere they to age should come,
Their uncle should possess their wealth!
   For so the will did run.

"Now, brother," said the dying man,
   "Look to my children dear;
Be good unto my boy and girl,
   No friends else have they here."

Their parents being dead and gone,
   The children home he takes,
And brings them both unto his house,
   Where much of them he makes.

[40]

He had not kept those pretty babes
   A twelvemonth and a day,
When, for their wealth, he did devise
   To make them both away.

      He bargained with two ruffians bold,
         Who were of savage mood,
      That they should take the children twain,
         And slay them in a wood.

            They prate and prattle pleasantly,
               While riding on the way,
            To those their wicked uncle hired
               These lovely babes to slay:

So that the pretty speech they had,
   Made the ruffian's heart relent;
And they that took the deed to do,
   Full sorely did repent.

      Yet one of them, more hard of heart,
         Did vow to do his charge,
      Because the wretch that hired him
         Had paid him very large.

         The other would not agree thereto,
            So here they fell at strife;
         With one another they did fight,
            About the children's life:

              And he that was of milder mood
                 Did slay the other there,
              Within an unfrequented wood;
                 The babes did quake for fear!

He took the children by the hand,
  While they for bread complain:
"Stay here," quoth he, "I'll bring ye bread,
  When I do come again."

      These pretty babes, with hand in hand,
        Went wandering up and down;
      But never more they saw the man
        Approaching from the town.

      Thus wandered these two pretty dears,
        Till death did end their grief;
      In one another's arms they died,
        Poor babes! past all relief.

No burial these innocents
  Of any man receives,
But Robin Redbreast lovingly
  Did cover them with leaves.

      The fellow that did take in hand
        These children for to kill,
      Was for a robbery judged to die,
        As was God's blessed will:

      And did confess the very truth,
        The which is here expressed;
      Their uncle died while he for debt
        Did long in prison rest.

Great A, little a.

Great A, little a, Bouncing B,
The cat's in the cupboard, and she can't see.

Monday's Bairn.

MONDAY'S bairn is fair of face,
Tuesday's bairn is full of grace,
Wednesday's bairn is full of woe,
Thursday's bairn has far to go,
Friday's bairn is loving and giving,
Saturday's bairn works hard for its living,
But the bairn that is born on the Sabbath day
Is bonny and blythe and good and gay.

There was an old Woman, and what do you think?

THERE was an old woman, and what do you think?
She lived upon nothing but victuals and drink:
Victuals and drink were the chief of her diet;
Yet this little old woman could never keep quiet.

She went to the baker, to buy her some bread,
And when she came home her old husband was dead;
She went to the clerk to toll the bell,
And when she came back her old husband was well.

Little Blue Betty.

LITTLE Blue Betty lived in a lane,
She sold good ale to gentlemen:
Gentlemen came every day,
And little Betty Blue hopped away.
She hopped upstairs to make her bed,
And she tumbled down and broke her head.

[43]

One old Oxford Ox.

ONE old Oxford ox opening oysters;
    Two tee-totums totally tired of trying to trot to Tedsbury;
    Three thick thumping tigers tickling trout;
Four fat friars fanning fainting fleas;
Five frippy Frenchmen foolishly fishing for flies;
Six sportsmen shooting snipes;
Seven Severn salmons swallowing shrimps;
Eight Englishmen eagerly examining Europe;
Nine nimble noblemen nibbling nonpareils;
Ten tinkers tinkling upon ten tin tinder-boxes with ten tenpenny
    tacks;
Eleven elephants elegantly equipt;
Twelve typographical topographers typically translating types.

The Queen of Hearts.

THE Queen of Hearts,
    She made some tarts,
    All on a summer's day;

The Knave of Hearts,
He stole those tarts,
    And took them clean away.

The King of Hearts
Called for the tarts,
    And beat the Knave full sore;

The Knave of Hearts
Brought back the tarts,
    And vowed he'd steal no more.

[44]

ELIZABETH CURTIS.

"THE QUEEN OF HEARTS, SHE MADE SOME TARTS"

Sing Song, merry go round.

SING song! merry go round,
   Here we go up to the moon, oh,
   Little Johnnie a penny has found,
And so we'll sing a tune, oh!
  What shall I buy?
  Johnnie did cry,
With the penny I've found
So bright and round?
What shall you buy?
A kite that will fly
Up to the moon, all through the sky!
But if, when it gets there,
It should stay in the air,
Or the man in the moon
Should open the door,
And take it in with his long, long paw,—
We should sing to another tune, oh!

I saw a Ship a-sailing.

I SAW a ship a-sailing,
   A-sailing on the sea;
   And it was full of pretty things
For baby and for me.

        There were comfits in the cabin,
          And apples in the hold;
        The sails were all of velvet,
          And the masts of beaten gold.

[46]

The four-and-twenty sailors
   That stood between the decks,
Were four-and-twenty white mice,
   With chains about their necks.

   The captain was a duck,
      With a packet on his back;
   And when the ship began to move,
      The captain said, "Quack! quack!"

Shoe the horse, and shoe the mare;
But let the little colt go bare.

The Song of five Toes.

1. This little pig went to market;
2. This little pig stayed at home;
3. This little pig had roast beef;
4. This little pig had none;
5. This little pig said, wee, wee, wee!
   I can't find my way home.

I had a little Dog.

I HAD a little dog, and his name was Blue Bell,
   I gave him some work, and he did it very well;
   I sent him upstairs to pick up a pin,
He stepped in the coal-scuttle up to the chin;

   I sent him to the garden to pick some sage,
   He tumbled down and fell in a rage;
   I sent him to the cellar to draw a pot of beer,
   He came up again and said there was none there.

The Piper and his Cow.

THERE was a Piper had a Cow,
    And he had naught to give her;
    He pulled out his pipes and played her a tune,
And bade the cow consider.

The Cow considered very well,
    And gave the Piper a penny,
And bade him play the other tune:
    "Corn rigs are bonny."

Ladybug, Ladybug.

LADYBUG, ladybug,
    Fly away home,
    Your house is on fire,
And your children will burn.

What Shoemaker?

WHAT shoemaker makes shoes without leather,
    With all the four elements put together?
    Fire and water, earth and air;
Every customer has two pair.
                (*A horse-shoer.*)

Hey, dorolot!

HEY, dorolot, dorolot!
    Hey, dorolay, dorolay!
    Hey, my bonny boat, bonny boat,
Hey, drag away, drag away!

I had a little Hobby-horse.

I HAD a little hobby-horse,
  And it was dapple grey;
  Its head was made of pea-straw,
Its tail was made of hay.

I sold it to an old woman
  For a copper groat;
And I'll not sing my song again
Without a new coat.

Round the Jingo-Ring.

HERE we go round the jingo-ring,
  The jingo-ring, the jingo-ring,
  Here we go round the jingo-ring,
With a merry-ma, merry-ma-tanzie.

  Twice about and then we fall,
  Then we fall, then we fall,
  Twice about and then we fall,
  With a merry-ma, merry-ma-tanzie.

    Choose your maidens all around,
    All around, all around,
    Choose your maidens all around,
    With a merry-ma, merry-ma-tanzie.

I do not like thee, Doctor Fell.

I DO not like thee, Doctor Fell,
  The reason why I cannot tell;
  But this I know, and know full well,
I do not like thee, Doctor Fell.

[49]

There was a Man, and he was mad.

THERE was a man and he was mad,
  And he jumped into a pea-swad;
  The pea-swad was over-full,
So he jumped into a roaring bull;
The roaring bull was over-fat,
So he jumped into a gentleman's hat;
The gentleman's hat was over-fine,
So he jumped into a bottle of wine;
The bottle of wine was over-dear,
So he jumped into a barrel of beer;
The barrel of beer was over-thick,
So he jumped into a club-stick;
The club-stick was over-narrow,
So he jumped into a wheelbarrow;
The wheelbarrow began to crack,
So he jumped on to a hay-stack;
The hay-stack began to blaze,
So he did nothing but cough and sneeze!

As I was going up Pippen Hill.

AS I was going up Pippen Hill,
  Pippen Hill was dirty;
  There I met a pretty miss,
And she dropped me a curtsey.

Little miss, pretty miss,
  Blessings light upon you!
If I had half-a-crown a day,
  I'd spend it all on you.

[50]

Cock a doodle doo!

COCK a doodle doo!
My dame has lost her shoe;
My master's lost his fiddling stick,
And don't know what to do.

Cock a doodle doo!
What is my dame to do?
Till master finds his fiddling stick,
She'll dance without her shoe.

Cock a doodle doo!
My dame has lost her shoe,
And master's found his fiddling stick,
Sing doodle doodle doo!

Cock a doodle doo!
My dame will dance with you.
While master fiddles his fiddling stick,
For dame and doodle doo.

Cock a doodle doo!
Dame has lost her shoe;
Gone to bed and scratched her head,
And can't tell what to do.

Little Willie Winkle.

LITTLE Willie Winkle runs through the town,
Upstairs and downstairs, in his nightgown,
Rapping at the window, crying through the lock,
"Are the children in their beds? for now it's eight o'clock."

There was an old Woman.

THERE was an old woman who lived in a shoe,
 She had so many children she didn't know what to do;
 She gave them some broth without any bread,
She whipped them all round, and sent them to bed.

Little brown Mouse.

PRETTY John Watts,
 We are troubled with rats,
 Will you drive them out of the house?
We have mice, too, in plenty,
That feast in the pantry;
But let them stay,
And nibble away:
What harm in a little brown mouse?

Pussy-cat sits by the fire.

PUSSY-CAT sits by the fire:
 How did she come there?
 In walks the little dog—
Says, "Pussy! are you there?
How do you do, Mistress Pussy?
Mistress Pussy, how d'ye do?"
"I thank you kindly, little dog,
 I fare as well as you!"

Willy Boy, where are you going?

WILLY boy, Willy boy, where are you going?
 I will go with you, if that I may.
 I'm going to the meadow to see them a mowing,
I'm going to help them make the hay.

"THERE WAS AN OLD WOMAN WHO LIVED IN A SHOE"

The Spider and the Fly.

"WILL you walk into my parlour?" said the spider to the
      fly,—
      " 'Tis the prettiest little parlour that ever you did spy.
The way into my parlour is up a winding stair;
And I have many curious things to show you when you're there."
"Oh no, no," said the little fly; "to ask me is in vain;
For who goes up your winding stair can ne'er come down
      again."

"I'm sure you must be weary, dear, with soaring up so high;
Will you rest upon my little bed?" said the spider to the fly.
"There are pretty curtains drawn around; the sheets are fine and
      thin;
And if you like to rest awhile, I'll snugly tuck you in!"
"Oh no, no," said the little fly; "for I've often heard it said,
They never, never wake again who sleep upon your bed!"

Said the cunning spider to the fly—"Dear friend, what can
      I do
To prove the warm affection I've always felt for you?
I have within my pantry good store of all that's nice;
I'm sure you're very welcome—will you please to take a slice?"
"Oh no, no," said the little fly, "kind sir, that cannot be;
I've heard what's in your pantry and I do not wish to see."

"Sweet creature," said the spider, "you're witty and you're wise.
How handsome are your gauzy wings, how brilliant are your
      eyes!
I have a little looking-glass upon my parlour shelf,
If you'll step in one moment, dear, you shall behold yourself."

"I thank you, gentle sir," she said, "for what you're pleased to
say,
And bidding you good-morning now, I'll call another day."

The spider turned him round about, and went into his den,
For well he knew the silly fly would soon come back again;
So he wove a subtle web in a little corner sly,
And set his table ready, to dine upon the fly.
Then he came out to his door again, and merrily did sing,—
"Come hither, hither, pretty fly, with the pearl and silver wing;
Your robes are green and purple—there's a crest upon your
head!
Your eyes are like the diamond bright, but mine are dull as
lead!"

Alas! alas! how very soon this silly little fly,
Hearing his wily, flattering words, came slowly flitting by.
With buzzing wings she hung aloft, then near and nearer
drew,
Thinking only of her brilliant eyes, her green and purple
hue—
Thinking only of her crested head—poor foolish thing! At
last,
Up jumped the cunning spider, and fiercely held her fast!
He dragged her up his winding stairs, into his dismal den,
Within his little parlour—but she ne'er came out again!

And now, dear little children, who may this story read,
To idle, silly flattering words, I pray you, ne'er give heed;
Unto an evil counsellor close heart, and ear, and eye,
And take a lesson from this tale of the Spider and the Fly.

Lucy Locket.

LUCY LOCKET lost her pocket,
   Kitty Fisher found it;
   Never a penny was there in it,
Save the binding round it.

Hickety, Pickety.

HICKETY, pickety, my black hen,
   She lays eggs for gentlemen;
   Gentlemen come every day
To see what my black hen doth lay.

Lady Bird, Lady Bird.

LADY bird, lady bird, fly away home,
   Your house is on fire, your children have flown.
   All but one, and her name is Ann,
And she has crept under the pudding-pan.

Sing Ivy.

MY father left me three acres of land,
   Sing ivy, sing ivy;
   My father left me three acres of land,
Sing holly, go whistle and ivy!

   I ploughed it with a ram's horn,
      Sing ivy, sing ivy;
   And sowed it all over with one pepper-corn,
      Sing holly, go whistle and ivy!

[56]

I harrowed it with a bramble bush,
    Sing ivy, sing ivy;
And reaped it with my little penknife,
    Sing holly, go whistle, and ivy!

    I got the mice to carry it to the barn,
        Sing ivy, sing ivy;
    And thrashed it with a goose's quill,
        Sing holly, go whistle, and ivy!

        I got the cat to carry it to the mill,
            Sing holly, go whistle, and ivy!
        The miller he swore he would have her paw,
        And the cat she swore she would scratch his face,
            Sing holly, go whistle, and ivy!

RIDDLE-ME, riddle-me, riddle-me-ree,
    Perhaps you can tell what this riddle may be:
    As deep as a house, as round as a cup,
And all the King's horses can't draw it up.
(*A well.*)

I love my Love.

I LOVE my love with an A, because he's Agreeable.
    I hate him because he's Avaricious.
    He took me to the Sign of the Acorn,
And treated me with Apples.
His name's Andrew,
And he lives at Arlington.
    (*This can be continued through the alphabet.*)

[57]

Peter, Peter, Pumpkin Eater.

PETER, Peter, Pumpkin Eater,
  Had a wife and couldn't keep her.
  He put her in a pumpkin shell,
And there he kept her very well.

Peter, Peter, Pumpkin Eater,
  Had another and didn't love her.
  Peter learned to read and spell,
  And then he loved her very well.

One, two, three.

ONE, two, three,
  I love coffee,
    And Billy loves tea.
How good you be,
One, two, three,
I love coffee,
And Billy loves tea.

Nose, Nose.

NOSE, nose, jolly red nose;
  And what gave thee that jolly red nose?
  Nutmegs and cinnamon, spices and cloves,
And they gave me this jolly red nose.

See-saw, sacaradown.

SEE-SAW, sacaradown,
  Which is the way to London town?
  One foot up, the other down,
This is the way to London town.

[58]

Two, three, and four Legs.

TWO legs sat upon three legs,
　　With one leg in his lap;
　　In comes four legs,
And runs away with one leg,
Up jumps two legs,
Catches up three legs,
Throws it after four legs,
And makes him bring back one leg.

Three Children.

THREE children sliding on the ice
Upon a summer's day,
　It so fell out, they all fell in,
The rest they ran away.

　　Now had these children been at home,
　　Or sliding on dry ground,
　　Ten thousand pounds to one penny
　　They had not all been drown'd.

　　　　You parents all that children have,
　　　　And you that have got none,
　　　　If you would have them safe abroad,
　　　　Pray keep them safe at home.

Pussy-cat, Pussy-cat.

PUSSY-CAT, pussy-cat, where have you been?
I've been up to London to look at the queen.
Pussy-cat, pussy-cat, what did you there?
I frightened a little mouse under the chair.

[59]

Little Robin Redbreast.

LITTLE Robin Redbreast sat upon a tree,
   Up went Pussy cat, and down went he;
   Down came Pussy cat, and away Robin ran;
Says little Robin Redbreast, "Catch me if you can."
Little Robin Redbreast jump'd upon a wall,
Pussy cat jump'd after him, and almost got a fall,
Little Robin chirp'd and sang, and what did Pussy say?
Pussy cat said "Mew," and Robin jump'd away.

Jack Sprat.

JACK SPRAT could eat no fat,
   His wife could eat no lean;
      And so, betwixt them both, [you see]
   They licked the platter clean.

Old King Cole.

OLD King Cole
   Was a merry old soul,
      And a merry old soul was he;
He called for his pipe,
And he called for his bowl,
And he called for his fiddlers three.
      Every fiddler, he had a fiddle,
      And a very fine fiddle had he;
      Twee tweedle dee, tweedle dee, went the fiddlers.
      Oh, there's none so rare,
      As can compare
      With King Cole and his fiddlers three!

"JACK SPRAT COULD EAT NO FAT"

There was a crooked Man.

THERE was a crooked man, and he went a crooked mile;
    He found a crooked sixpence against a crooked stile;
    He bought a crooked cat, which caught a crooked mouse;
And they all lived together in a little crooked house.

For every Evil under the Sun.

FOR every evil under the sun,
    There is a remedy, or there is none,
    If there be one, seek till you find it;
If there be none, never mind it.

There were two Blackbirds.

THERE were two blackbirds
    Sitting on a hill,
    The one named Jack,
    The other named Jill;
Fly away, Jack!
Fly away, Jill!
Come again, Jack!
Come again, Jill!

Four and twenty-Tailors.

FOUR and twenty tailors went to kill a snail,
    The best man among them durst not touch her tail;
    She put out her horns like a little Kyloe cow,
Run, tailors, run, or she'll kill you all e'en now.

Playmates.

PRAY, playmates agree.
  E, F, and G,
  Well, so it shall be.
J, K, and L,
In peace we will dwell.
M, N, and O,
To play let us go.
P, Q, R and S,
Love may we possess.
W, X, and Y,
Will not quarrel or die.
Z, and amperse—and,
Go to school at command.

Dickery, dickery, dare.

DICKERY, dickery, dare,
  The pig flew up in the air;
  The man in brown soon brought him down,
Dickery, dickery, dare.

Little Tee Wee.

LITTLE Tee Wee,
  He went to sea
  In an open boat;
And while afloat
The little boat bended,
And my story's ended.

[63]

Kitty alone and I.

THERE was a frog lived in a well,
   Kitty alone, Kitty alone;
   There was a frog lived in a well;
Kitty alone and I!

    There was a frog lived in a well;
    And a farce * mouse in a mill,
    Cock me carry, Kitty alone,
      Kitty alone and I.

    This frog he would a-wooing ride,
      Kitty alone, &c.
    This frog he would a-wooing ride,
    And on a snail he got astride,
      Cock me carry, &c.

He rode till he came to my Lady Mouse Hall,
   Kitty alone, &c.
He rode till he came to my Lady Mouse Hall,
And there he did both knock and call,
   Cock me carry, &c.

    Quoth he, "Miss Mouse, I'm come to thee,"—
      Kitty alone, &c.
    Quoth he, "Miss Mouse, I'm come to thee,
    To see if thou canst fancy me."
      Cock me carry, &c.

* merry

[64]

Quoth she, "Answer I'll give you none"—
  Kitty alone, &c.
Quoth she, "Answer I'll give you none
Until my Uncle Rat come home."
  Cock me carry, &c.

            And when her Uncle Rat came home,
              Kitty alone, &c.
            And when her Uncle Rat came home:
            "Who's been here since I've been gone?"
              Cock me carry, &c.

"Sir, there's been a worthy gentleman"—
  Kitty alone, &c.
"Sir, there's been a worthy gentleman—
That's been here since you've been gone."
  Cock me carry, &c.

        The frog he came whistling through the brook,
          Kitty alone, &c.
        The frog he came whistling through the brook,
        And there he met with a dainty duck.
          Cock me carry, &c.

          This duck she swallowed him up with a pluck,
            Kitty alone, Kitty alone;
          This duck she swallowed him up with a pluck,
          So there's an end of my history-book.
            Cock me carry, Kitty alone,
            Kitty alone and I.
              [65]

Oh, deary, deary me.

THERE was an old woman, as I've heard tell,
She went to market her eggs for to sell;
She went to market all on a market day,
And she fell asleep on the King's highway.

There came by a pedlar, whose name was Stout—
He cut her petticoats all round about;
He cut her petticoats up to the knees,
Which made the old woman to shiver and freeze.

When this little woman first did wake,
She began to shiver and she began to shake,
She began to wonder and she began to cry,
"Oh! deary, deary me, this is none of I!

"But if it be I, as I do hope it be,
I have a little dog at home, and he'll know me;
If it be I, he'll wag his little tail,
And if it be not I, he'll loudly bark and wail."

Home went the little woman all in the dark;
Up got the little dog, and he began to bark;
He began to bark, so she began to cry,
"Oh! deary, deary me, this is none of I!"

Leg over Leg.

LEG over leg,
As the dog went to Dover;
When he came to a stile,
Jump! he went over.

Bobby Shaftoe.

BOBBY SHAFTOE'S gone to sea,
    Silver buckles on his knee;
    He'll come back and marry me,
Bonny Bobby Shaftoe!

Bobby Shaftoe's young and fair,
Combing down his yellow hair,
He's my love for evermore,
Bonny Bobby Shaftoe.

Billy, Billy, come and play.

BILLY, Billy, come and play,
    While the sun shines bright as day."

"Yes, my Polly, so I will,
For I love to please you still."

"Billy, Billy, have you seen,
Sam and Betsy on the green?"

"Yes, my Poll, I saw them pass,
Skipping o'er the new-mown grass."

"Billy, Billy, come along,
And I will sing a pretty song."

"O then, Polly, I'll make haste,
Not one moment will I waste,
But will come and hear you sing,
And my fiddle I will bring."
[67]

Sing a Song of Sixpence.

SING a song if sixpence,
    Pocket full of rye;
    Four and twenty blackbirds
Baked in a pie.

When the pie was opened
The birds began to sing—
Oh, wasn't that a dainty dish
To set before the king?

As little Jenny Wren.

AS little Jenny Wren
    Was sitting by the shed,
    She waggled with her tail,
And nodded with her head.
She waggled with her tail,
And nodded with her head,
As little Jenny Wren
Was sitting by the shed.

Hot-cross Buns!

HOT-CROSS Buns!
    Hot-cross Buns!
    One a penny, two a penny
Hot-cross Buns!

Hot-cross Buns!
Hot-cross Buns!
If ye have no daughters,
    Give them to your sons.

[68]

"SING A SONG OF SIXPENCE"

See, Saw, Margery Daw.

SEE, Saw, Margery Daw,
  Sold her bed and lay upon straw;
  Was not she a dirty slut,
To sell her bed and lie in the dirt!

Lock and Key.

I AM a gold lock.
  I am a gold key.
  I am a silver lock.
I am a silver key.
I am a brass lock.
I am a brass key.
I am a lead lock.
I am a lead key.
I am a monk lock.
I am a monk key!

High diddle ding.

HIGH diddle ding,
  Did you hear the bells ring?
  The Parliament soldiers are gone to the King;
Some they did laugh, some they did cry,
To see the Parliament soldiers pass by.

[70]

Jenny Wren.

IT was on a merry time,
When Jenny Wren was young,
So neatly as she dressed,
And so sweetly as she sung.

Robin Redbreast lost his heart,
He was a gallant bird;
He doffed his hat to Jenny,
And thus to her he said:

"My dearest Jenny Wren,
If you will but be mine,
You shall dine on cherry pie
And drink nice currant wine.

"I'll dress you like a goldfinch,
Or like a peacock gay;
So, if you'll have me, Jenny,
Let us appoint the day."

Jenny blushed behind her fan,
And thus declared her mind:
"Then let it be to-morrow, Bob—
I take your offer kind.

"Cherry pie is very good,
So is currant wine;
But I'll wear my russet gown
And never dress too fine."

[71]

Robin rose up early,
  At the break of day;
He flew to Jenny Wren's house
  To sing a roundelay.

        He met the Cock and Hen,
          And bade the Cock declare
        This was his wedding day
          With Jenny Wren the fair.

The Cock then blew his horn,
  To let the neighbours know
This was Robin's wedding day,
  And they might see the show.

At first came Parson Rook,
  With his spectacles and band;
And one of Mother Hubbard's books,
  He held within his hand.

        Then followed him the Lark,
          For he could sweetly sing,
        And he was to be the clerk
          At Cock Robin's wedding.

                He sang of Robin's love
                  For little Jenny Wren;
                And when he came unto the end,
                  Then he began again.

                        The Goldfinch came on next,
                          To give away the bride;
                        The Linnet, being bridesmaid,
                          Walked by Jenny's side;

And as she was a-walking,
　Said, "Upon my word,
I think that your Cock Robin
　Is a very pretty bird."

　　　The Blackbird and the Thrush,
　　　　And charming Nightingale,
　　　Whose sweet songs sweetly echo
　　　　Through every grove and dale;

　　　　　　The Sparrow and the Tomtit
　　　　　　　And many more were there,
　　　　　　All came to see the wedding
　　　　　　　Of Jenny Wren the fair.

The Bullfinch walked by Robin,
　And thus to him did say:
"Pray mark, friend Robin Redbreast,
　That Goldfinch dressed so gay.

　　　"What though her gay apparel
　　　　Becomes her very well,
　　　Yet Jenny's modest dress and look
　　　　Must bear away the bell!"

　　　　　Then came the bride and bridegroom;
　　　　　　Quite plainly was she dressed,
　　　　　And blushed so much, her cheeks were
　　　　　　As red as Robin's breast.

　　　　　　But Robin cheered her up;
　　　　　　　"My pretty Jen," says he,
　　　　　　"We're going to be married,
　　　　　　　And happy we shall be."

[73]

"Oh," then says Parson Rook,
  "Who gives this maid away?"
"I do," says the Goldfinch,
  "And her fortune I will pay:

    "Here's a bag of grain of many sorts,
      And other things beside;
    Now happy be the bridegroom,
      And happy be the bride!"

        "And you will have her, Robin,
          To be your wedded wife?"
        "Yes, I will," says Robin,
          "And love her all my life!"

        "And you will have him, Jenny,
          Your husband now to be?"
        "Yes, I will," says Jenny,
          "And love him heartily."

    Then on her finger fair
      Cock Robin put the ring;
    "You're married now," says Parson Rook,
      While the Lark aloud did sing:

        "Happy be the bridegroom,
          And happy be the bride!
        And may not man, nor bird, nor beast,
          This happy pair divide!"

            The birds were asked to dine;
              Not Jenny's friends alone,
            But every pretty songster
              That had Cock Robin known.

[74]

They had a cherry pie,
    Besides some currant wine,
And every guest brought something,
    That sumptuous they might dine.

            Now they all sat or stood,
              To eat and to drink;
            And every one said what
              He happened to think.

They each took a bumper,   The dinner-things removed,
    And drank to the pair,   They all began to sing;
Cock Robin the bridegroom,   And soon they made the place
    And Jenny the fair.   For a mile around to ring.

        The concert it was fine,
           And every birdie tried
        Who best should sing for Robin
        And Jenny Wren the bride.

            When in came the Cuckoo,
              And made a great rout;
            He caught hold of Jenny,
              And pulled her about.

                Cock Robin was angry,
                  And so was the Sparrow,
                Who fetched in a hurry
                  His bow and his arrow.

His aim then he took,
  But he took it not right,
His skill was not good,
  Or he shot in a fright;

      For the Cuckoo he missed,
        But Cock Robin he killed!
      And all the birds mourned
        That his blood was so spilled.

Where are you going?

WHERE are you going, my pretty maid?"
    "I'm going a-milking, sir," she said.
    "May I go with you, my pretty maid?"
"You're kindly welcome, sir," she said.
"What is your father, my pretty maid?"
"My father's a farmer, sir," she said.
"What is your fortune, my pretty maid?"
"My face is my fortune, sir," she said.
"Then I can't marry you, my pretty maid!"
"Nobody asked you, sir!" she said.

A Thatcher of Thatchwood.

A THATCHER of Thatchwood went to Thatchet a-thatch-
      ing;
    Did a thatcher of Thatchwood go to Thatchet a-thatch-
      ing?
If a thatcher of Thatchwood went to Thatchet a-thatching,
Where's the thatching the thatcher of Thatchwood has
    thatched?

"WHERE ARE YOU GOING, MY PRETTY MAID?"

Where should a Baby rest?

WHERE should a baby rest?
　　Where but on its mother's arm—
　　Where can a baby lie
Half so safe from every harm?
　　Lulla, lulla, lullaby,
　　Softly sleep, my baby;
　　Lulla, lulla, lullaby,
　　Soft, soft, my baby.

　　　　Nestle there, my lovely one!
　　　　Press to mine thy velvet cheek;
　　　　Sweetly coo, and smile, and look,
　　　　All the love thou canst not speak.
　　　　　Lulla, lulla, lullaby,
　　　　　Softly sleep, my baby;
　　　　　Lulla, lulla, lullaby,
　　　　　Soft, soft, my baby.

A Riddle.

THERE was a little green house
　　And in the little green house
　　There was a little brown house,
And in the little brown house
There was a little yellow house,
And in the little yellow house
There was a little white house,
And in the little white house
There was a little heart.
　　　　　　　(*A walnut.*)

[78]

Here we go round the Mulberry-bush.

HERE we go round the mulberry-bush,
   The mulberry-bush, the mulberry-bush,
   Here we go round the mulberry-bush,
On a cold and frosty morning.

   This is the way we wash our clothes,
   Wash our clothes, wash our clothes,
   This is the way we wash our clothes,
   On a cold and frosty morning.

This is the way we iron our clothes,
Iron our clothes, iron our clothes,
This is the way we iron our clothes,
On a cold and frosty morning.

This is the way we sweep our rooms,
Sweep our rooms, sweep our rooms,
This is the way we sweep our rooms,
On a cold and frosty morning.

   This is the way we mend our shoes,
   Mend our shoes, mend our shoes,
   This is the way we mend our shoes,
   On a cold and frosty morning.

      This is the way we wash our hands,
      Wash our hands, wash our hands,
      This is the way we wash our hands,
      On a cold and frosty morning.

[79]

This is the way we do our hair,
Do our hair, do our hair,
This is the way we do our hair,
On a cold and frosty morning.

This is the way we go to school,
Go to school, go to school,
This is the way we go to school,
On a cold and frosty morning.

This is the way we come home from school,
Home from school, home from school,
This is the way we come home from school,
On a cold and frosty morning.

Curly Locks.

CURLY locks! curly locks! wilt thou be mine?
Thou shalt not wash dishes, nor yet feed the swine;
But sit on a cushion and sew a fine seam,
And feed upon strawberries, sugar, and cream!

My little Brother.

I LOVE you well, my little brother,
And you are fond of me;
Let us be kind to one another,
As brothers ought to be.
You shall learn to play with me,
And learn to use my toys;
And then I think that we shall be
Two happy little boys.

[80]

The Man in the Moon.

THE man in the moon came down too soon,
And asked his way to Norwich;
He went by the south and burnt his mouth
With eating cold plum-porridge.

I'll sing you a Song.

I'LL sing you a song,
Though not very long,
Yet I think it as pretty as any;
Put your hand in your purse,
You'll never be worse,
And give the poor singer a penny.

As soft as Silk.

AS soft as silk, as white as milk,
As bitter as gall, a strong wall,
And a green coat covers me all.
(*A walnut.*)

A Carrion Crow.

A CARRION crow sat on an oak,
Fol de riddle, lol de riddle, hi ding do,
Watching a tailor shape his coat;
Sing heigh ho, the carrion crow,
Fol de riddle, lol de riddle, hi ding do.

HERE goes my lord
A trot, a trot, a trot, a trot!
Here goes my lady
A canter, a canter, a canter, a canter!

Fiddle cum fee.

A CAT came fiddling out of a barn,
With a pair of bagpipes under her arm;
She could sing nothing but fiddle cum fee,
The mouse has married the bumble-bee!
Pipe, cat; dance, mouse:
We'll have a wedding at our good house.

Brow brinky.

BROW brinky,
Eye kinky,
Chin choppy,
Nose noppy,
Cheek cherry,
Mouth merry.

There was a little Man.

THERE was a little man and he had a little gun,
And his bullets were made of lead,
He shot John Sprig through the middle of his wig,
And knocked it right off his head.

[82]

Buzz and hum.

BUZZ, quoth the blue fly,
   Hum, quoth the bee,
   Buzz and hum they cry,
 And so do we:
In his ear, in his nose, thus, do you see?
He ate the dormouse, else it was he.

There was a little Guinea-Pig.

THERE was a little Guinea-pig,
   Who, being little, was not big;
   He always walked upon his feet,
And never fasted when he eat.

When from a place he ran away,
He never at that place did stay;
And while he ran, as I am told,
He ne'er stood still for young or old.

He often squeak'd and sometimes vi'lent,
And when he squeak'd he ne'er was silent;
Though ne'er instructed by a cat,
He knew a mouse was not a rat.

One day, as I am certified,
He took a whim and fairly died;
And, as I'm told by men of sense,
He never has been living since.

[83]

Sing, sing, what shall I sing?

SING, sing, what shall I sing?
  The cat has ate the pudding-string!
  Do, do, what shall I do?
The cat has bit it quite in two.

A Diller, a Dollar.

A DILLER, a dollar,
  A ten o'clock scholar,
    What makes you come so soon?
  You used to come at ten o'clock,
  But now you come at noon.

The Rose is red.

THE rose is red, the violet blue;
  Sugar is sweet—and so are you.
  These are the words you bade me say
For a pair of new gloves on Easter day.

Fiddle-De-Dee.

FIDDLE-DE-DEE, fiddle-de-dee,
  The fly shall marry the humble-bee.
  They went to the church, and married was she,
The fly has married the humble-bee.

[84]

"A DILLER, A DOLLAR, A TEN O'CLOCK SCHOLAR"

Para-mara, dictum, domine.

I HAVE four sisters beyond the sea,
    Para-mara, dictum, domine.
    And they did send four presents to me,
    Partum, quartum, paradise, tempum,
    Para-mara, dictum, domine!

The first it was a bird without e'er a bone;
    Para-mara, dictum, &c.
The second was a cherry without e'er a stone;
    Para-mara, dictum, &c.

The third it was a blanket without e'er a thread,
    Para-mara, dictum, &c.
The fourth it was a book which no man could read;
    Partum, quartum, &c.

How can there be a bird without e'er a bone?
    Para-mara, dictum, &c.
How can there be a cherry without e'er a stone?
    Partum, quartum, &c.

How can there be a blanket without e'er a thread?
    Para-mara, dictum, &c.
How can there be a book which no man can read?
    Partum, quartum, &c.

When the bird's in the shell, there is no bone;
    Para-mara, dictum, &c.
When the cherry's in the bud, there is no stone;
    Partum, quartum, &c.

When the blanket's in the fleece, there is no thread;
  Para-mara, dictum, &c.
When the book's in the press, no man can read;
  Partum, quartum, &c.

A Man of Words and not of Deeds.

A MAN of words and not of deeds,
    Is like a garden full of weeds;
    And when the weeds begin to grow,
It's like a garden full of snow;
And when the snow begins to fall,
It's like a bird upon the wall;
And when the bird away does fly,
It's like an eagle in the sky;
And when the sky begins to roar,
It's like a lion at the door;
And when the door begins to crack,
It's like a stick across your back;
And when your back begins to smart,
It's like a penknife in your heart;
And when your heart begins to bleed.
You're dead, and dead, and dead, indeed.

There was an old Soldier of Bister.

THERE was an old soldier of Bister
    Went walking one day with his sister,
    When a cow at one poke
Tossed her into an oak,
Before the old gentleman missed her.

[87]

St. Swithin's Day.

ST. SWITHIN'S DAY, if thou dost rain,
 For forty days it will remain:
 St. Swithin's Day, if thou be fair,
For forty days 'twill rain na mair.

———

If Wishes were Horses.

IF wishes were horses,
 Beggars would ride;
 If turnips were watches,
I would wear one by my side.

———

IN fir tar is,
 In oak none is.
 In mud eel is,
In clay none is.
Goat eat ivy,
Mare eat oats.

There was an old Woman tossed up in a Basket.

THERE was an old woman tossed up in a basket,
 Seventy times as high as the moon.
 What she did there I could not but ask it,
For in her hand she carried a broom.

  "Old woman, old woman, old woman," said I,
  "Oh whither, oh whither, oh whither so high?"
  "To sweep the cobwebs off the sky,
  And I shall be back again by and by."

What are little Boys made of?

WHAT are little boys made of, made of,
What are little boys made of?
Snaps and snails, and puppydogs' tails;
And that's what little boys are made of, made of.

What are little girls made of, made of,
What are little girls made of?
Sugar and spice, and all that's nice;
And that's what little girls are made of, made of.

Solomon Grundy.

SOLOMON GRUNDY,
Born on a Monday,
Christened on Tuesday,
Married on Wednesday,
Took ill on Thursday,
Worse on Friday,
Died on Saturday,
Buried on Sunday:
This is the end
Of Solomon Grundy.

My Maid Mary.

MY maid Mary she minds her dairy,
While I go a-hoeing and mowing each morn;
Merrily run the reel and the little spinning-wheel
Whilst I am singing and mowing my corn.

Mary, Mary, quite contrary.

MARY, Mary, quite contrary,
    How does your garden grow?
    Silver bells and cockle shells
And pretty maids all in a row.

The Lion and the Unicorn.

THE lion and the unicorn
    Were fighting for the crown;
    The lion beat the unicorn
All round about the town.
Some gave them white bread,
    And some gave them brown;
Some gave them plum-cake,
    And sent them out of town.

There was a Man of our Town.

THERE was a man of our town,
    And he was wondrous wise,
    He jump'd into a bramble bush,
And scratch'd out both his eyes:
But when he saw his eyes were out,
    With all his might and main
He jump'd into another hedge,
    And scratch'd 'em in again.

If all the World were Water.

IF all the world were water,
  And all the sea were ink,
What should we do for bread and cheese?
What should we do for drink?

He that would thrive.

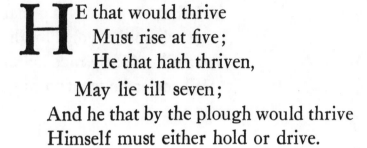

HE that would thrive
    Must rise at five;
    He that hath thriven,
  May lie till seven;
And he that by the plough would thrive
Himself must either hold or drive.

Pease Porridge hot.

PEASE porridge hot,
    Pease porridge cold,
    Pease porridge in the pot
  Nine days old.

What a fine Bird I be.

RIDDLE me, riddle me, ree,
  A hawk sate up on a tree;
  And he says to himself, says he,
Oh dear! what a fine bird I be!

———

FORMED long ago, yet made to-day,
  Employed while others sleep;
  What few would like to give away,
Nor any wish to keep.

(*A bed.*)

Good People all, of every sort.

GOOD people all, of every sort,
    Give ear unto my song:
And if you find it wondrous short,
It cannot hold you long.

In Islington there was a man,
    Of whom the world might say,
That still a Godly race he ran,
    Whene'er he went to pray.

A kind and gentle heart he had,
    To comfort friends and foes;
The naked every day he clad,
    When he put on his clothes.

And in that town a dog was found:
    As many dogs there be—
Both mongrel, puppy, whelp, and hound,
    And curs of low degree.

This dog and man at first were friends,
    But, when a pique began,
The dog, to gain some private ends,
    Went mad, and bit the man.

Around from all the neighbouring streets
    The wondering neighbours ran;
And swore the dog had lost his wits,
    To bite so good a man.

The wound it seemed both sore and sad
  To every Christian eye;
And while they swore the dog was mad,
  They swore the man would die.

But soon a wonder came to light,
  That showed the rogues they lied—
The man recovered of the bite;
  The dog it was that died.

Robert Barnes, Fellow fine.

ROBERT BARNES, fellow fine,
  Can you shoe this horse of mine?'
"Yes, good Sir, that I can,
As well as any other man;
There's a nail, and there's a prod,
And now, good Sir, your horse is shod."

Bye, Baby Bunting.

BYE, Baby Bunting,
  Father's gone a-hunting,
  To get a little rabbit skin
To wrap the Baby Bunting in.

The Man in the Wilderness.

THE man in the wilderness asked me,
  How many strawberries grew in the sea?
  I answered him, as I thought good,
As many as red herrings grew in the wood.

[93]

Hark! Hark! the Dogs do bark.

HARK! Hark! the dogs do bark,
  The beggars have come to town;
  Some in rags, and some in tags,
And some in velvet gowns.

This is the way the Ladies ride.

THIS is the way the ladies ride;
  Tri, tre, tre, tree,
  Tri, tre, tre, tree!
This is the way the ladies ride,
  Tri tre, tre, tre, tri-tre-tre-tree!

  This is the way the gentlemen ride;
    Gallop-a-trot,
    Gallop-a-trot!
  This is the way the gentlemen ride;
    Gallop-a-gallop-a-trot!

      This is the way the farmers ride;
        Hobbledy-hoy,
        Hobbledy-hoy!
      This is the way the farmers ride,
        Hobbledy hobbledy-hoy!

Ding, dong, darrow.

DING, dong, darrow,
  The cat and the sparrow;
  The little dog has burnt his tail,
And he shall be hanged to-morrow.

[94]

"HARK! HARK! THE DOGS DO BARK"

Robin the Bobbin.

ROBIN the Bobbin, the big bouncing Ben,
    He ate more meat than fourscore men;
    He ate a cow, he ate a calf,
He ate a butcher and a half;
He ate a church, he ate a steeple,
He ate the priest and all the people!

Here's Sulky Sue.

HERE'S Sulky Sue,
    What shall we do?
    Turn her face to the wall
Till she comes to.

Little Nancy Etticoat.

LITTLE Nancy Etticoat
    In a white petticoat
    And a red nose;
The longer she stands
The shorter she grows.

The Days of the Month.

THIRTY days hath September,
    April, June and November;
    February has twenty-eight alone,
All the rest have thirty-one,
Excepting leap-year, that's the time
When February's days are twenty-nine.

[96]

Twinkle, twinkle, little Star.

TWINKLE, twinkle, little star,
How I wonder what you are,
Up above the world so high,
Like a diamond in the sky.

When the blazing sun is gone,
When he nothing shines upon,
Then you show your little light,
Twinkle, twinkle, all the night.

Then the traveller in the dark
Thanks you for your tiny spark;
How could he see where to go,
If you did not twinkle so?

In the dark blue sky you keep,
Often through my curtains peep,
For you never shut your eye,
Till the sun is in the sky.

As your bright and tiny spark
Lights the traveller in the dark,
Though I know not what you are,
Twinkle, twinkle, little star.

Queen Anne, Queen Anne.

QUEEN ANNE, Queen Anne, you sit in the sun,
As fair as a lily, as white as a wand.
I send you three letters, and pray read one,
You must read one, if you can't read all,
So pray, Miss or Master, throw up the ball.

[97]

A little old Man and I fell out.

A LITTLE old man and I fell out:
How shall we bring this matter about?
Bring it about as well as you can—
Get you gone, you little old man!

Tell-Tale-Tit.

TELL-TALE-TIT,
Your tongue shall be slit,
And all the little puppy dogs
Shall have a little bit.

Gunpowder Treason.

PLEASE to remember
The Fifth of November
Gunpowder treason and plot;
I know no reason
Why gunpowder treason
Should ever be forgot.

Tommy Snooks and Betsey Brooks.

AS Tommy Snooks and Betsey Brooks
Were walking out one Sunday,
Said Tommy Snooks to Betsey Brooks,
To-morrow will be Monday.

[98]

Cold and raw.

COLD and raw the north wind doth blow,
　　Bleak in a morning early;
　　All the hills are covered with snow,
And winter's now come fairly.

See a Pin and pick it up.

SEE a pin and pick it up,
　　All the day you'll have good luck;
　　See a pin and let it lay,
Bad luck you'll have all the day.

The King of France.

THE King of France went up the hill,
　　With twenty thousand men;
　　The King of France came down the hill,
And ne'er went up again.

Taffy was a Welshman.

TAFFY was a Welshman, Taffy was a thief,
　　Taffy came to my house and stole a leg of beef;
　　I went to Taffy's house, Taffy wasn't home;
Taffy came to my house and stole a marrow bone.
I went to Taffy's house, Taffy was in bed;
I took the marrow-bone and beat Taffy's head.

[99]

Mary had a little Lamb.

MARY had a little lamb,
   Its fleece was white as snow;
   And everywhere that Mary went
The lamb was sure to go.

      It followed her to school one day,
         It was against the rule,
      And made the children laugh and play
         To see a lamb at school.

And so the teacher turned him out,
   But still he lingered near,
And waited patiently about
   Till Mary did appear.

      And then he ran to her, and laid
         His head upon her arm,
      As if he said, "I'm not afraid,
         You'll shield me from all harm."

         "What makes the lamb love Mary so?"
            The eager children cry.
         "Why, Mary loves the lamb, you know,"
            The teacher did reply.

JACK, be nimble,
   Jack, be quick.
   Jack ran off with the pudding-stick.

There was an old Woman called Nothing-at-all.

THERE was an old woman called Nothing-at-all,
 Who rejoiced in a dwelling exceedingly small:
 A man stretched his mouth to its utmost extent,
And down at one gulp house and old woman went.

Higgledy, Piggledy.

HIGGLEDY, piggledy, my black hen,
 She lays eggs for gentlemen;
 Sometimes nine, and sometimes ten,
Higgledy, piggledy, my black hen.

I'll tell you a Story.

I'LL tell you a story
 About Mary Morey,
 And now my story's begun.
 I'll tell you another,
 About her brother,
 And now my story's done.

Young Lambs to sell.

YOUNG Lambs to sell!
 Young Lambs to sell!
 If I'd as much money as I can tell,
I never would cry—Young Lambs to sell!

Robert Rowley.

ROBERT ROWLEY rolled a round roll round,
 A round roll Robert Rowley rolled round;
 Where rolled the round roll Robert Rowley rolled round?

Tom, Tom, the Piper's Son.

TOM, Tom, the piper's son,
   He learned to play when he was young,
   But all the tune that he could play,
Was "Over the hills and far away."
Over the hills, and a great way off,
And the wind will blow my top-knot off.

Now Tom with his pipe made such a noise,
That he pleased both the girls and boys,
And they stopped to hear him play,
"Over the hills and far away."

Tom with his pipe did play with such skill,
That those who heard him could never keep still;
Whenever they heard they began for to dance,
Even pigs on their hind legs would after him prance.

As Dolly was milking the cow one day,
Tom took out his pipe and began for to play;
So Doll and the cow danced "the Cheshire round,"
Till the pail was broke, and the milk ran on the ground.

He met old Dame Trot with a basket of eggs,
He used his pipe, and she used her legs;
She danced about till the eggs were all broke,
She began for to fret, but he laughed at the joke.

He saw a cross fellow was beating an ass,
Heavy laden with pots, pans, dishes and glass;
He took out his pipe and played them a tune,
And the jackass's load was lightened full soon.

[102]

"TOM, TOM, THE PIPER'S SON, HE LEARNED TO PLAY WHEN HE WAS YOUNG"

HERE am I, little jumping Joan;
　　When nobody's with me, I'm always alone.

My Father he died.

MY father he died, but I can't tell you how,
　　He left me six horses to drive in my plough:
　　With my wing wang waddle oh,
Jack sing saddle oh,
Blowsey boys buble oh,
Under the broom.

　　I sold my six horses, and I bought me a cow,
　　I'd fain have made a fortune, but did not know how:
　　　　With my wing wang waddle oh,
　　　　Jack sing saddle oh,
　　　　Blowsey boys buble oh,
　　　　Under the broom.

I sold my cow, and I bought me a calf;
I'd fain have made a fortune, but lost the best half;
　　With my wing wang waddle oh,
　　Jack sing saddle oh,
　　Blowsey boys buble oh,
　　Under the broom.

　　I sold my calf, and I bought me a cat;
　　A pretty thing she was, in my chimney corner sat:
　　　　With my wing wang waddle oh,
　　　　Jack sing saddle oh,
　　　　Blowsey boys buble oh,
　　　　Under the broom.

[104]

I sold my cat, and bought me a mouse;
He carried fire in his tail, and burnt down my house:
    With my wing wang waddle **oh,**
    Jack sing saddle oh,
    Blowsey boys buble **oh,**
    Under the broom.

Come hither, sweet Robin.

COME hither, sweet robin,
    And be not afraid,
      I would not hurt even a feather;
Come hither, sweet Robin,
    And pick up some bread,
To feed you this very cold weather.

I don't mean to frighten you,
    Poor little thing,
    And pussy-cat is not behind me;
So hop about pretty,
    And drop down your wing,
    And pick up some crumbs,
      And don't mind me.

I had a little Hen.

I HAD a little hen, the prettiest ever seen,
    She washed up the dishes, and kept the house clean;
    She went to the mill to fetch me some flour,
She brought it home in less than an hour;
She baked me my bread, she brewed me my ale,
She sat by the fire and told me a fine tale.

One, two, buckle my Shoe.

ONE, two,
Buckle my shoe;

Three, four,
Shut the door;

Five, six,
Pick up sticks;

Seven, eight,
Lay them straight;

Nine, ten,
A good fat hen;

Eleven, twelve,
Who will delve?

Thirteen, fourteen,
Maids a-courting;

Fifteen, sixteen,
Maids in the kitchen;

Seventeen, eighteen,
Maids a-waiting;

Nineteen, twenty,
My plate's empty.

Doctor Foster.

DOCTOR FOSTER went to Glo'ster,
In a shower of rain;
He stepped in a puddle, up to his middle,
And never went there again.

[106]

"ONE, TWO, BUCKLE MY SHOE"

The grey Goose is gone.

A FOX went out in a hungry plight
    And begged of the moon to give him light,
    For he had a long way to travel that night
Before he reached his Den O!
        Den O! Den O!
For he had a long way to travel that night
Before he reached his Den O!

At last he came to the farmer's yard
Where the ducks and geese declared it hard
That their nerves should be shaken, and their rest be marred
    By a visit from Mr. Fox O!
        Fox O! Fox O!
That their nerves should be shaken, and their rest be marred
    By a visit from Mr. Fox O!

He seized the grey goose by the sleeve,
Says he, Mrs. Goose, and by your leave,
I'll carry you off without reprieve,
    And take you away to my Den O!
        Den O! Den O!
I'll carry you off without reprieve,
    And take you away to my Den O!

Old Mrs. Flipper Flapper jumped out of bed,
And out of the window she popped her head,
Crying John, John, John, the grey goose is gone,
    And the Fox is off to his Den O!
        Den O! Den O!
Crying John, John, John, the grey goose is gone,
    And the Fox is off to his Den O!

Then John went up to the top of the hill,
And he blew a blast both loud and shrill.
Says the Fox, that's very pretty music, still
 I'd rather be in my Den O!
 Den O! Den O!
Says the Fox, that's very pretty music, still
 I'd rather be in my Den O!

At last Mr. Fox got home to his den,
To his dear little foxes, eight, nine, ten,
Says he, we're in luck, here's a big fat duck
 With his legs all dangling down O!
 Down O! Down O!
Says he, we're in luck, here's a big fat duck
 With his legs all dangling down O!

Then Mr. Fox sat down with his wife,
They did very well without fork and knife.
They never ate a better duck in all their life,
 And the little ones picked the bones O!
 Bones O! Bones O!
They never ate a better duck in all their life,
 And the little ones picked the bones O!

Poor Babes in the Wood.

MY dear, do you know,
 How a long time ago,
 Two poor little children,
 Whose names I don't know,
Were stolen away, on a fine summer's day,
And left in a wood, as I've heard people say?

And when it was night,
So sad was their plight,
The sun it went down,
And the moon gave no light.
They sobbed and they sighed, and they bitterly cried,
And the poor little things, they lay down and died.

And when they were dead,
The Robins so red
Brought strawberry-leaves
And over them spread;
And all the day long
They sung them this song:
"Poor babes in the wood!   Poor babes in the wood!
And don't you remember the babes in the wood?"

Little Tommy Tucker.

LITTLE Tommy Tucker,
   Sing for your supper:
   What shall I eat?
White bread and butter.
How shall I cut it
Without any knife?
How shall I marry
Without any wife?

My Mammy's Maid.

DINGTY, diddledy, my mammy's maid,
   She stole oranges, I'm afraid;
   Some in her pockets, some in her sleeve,
She stole oranges, I do believe.

Over the Water, and over the Sea.

OVER the water, and over the sea,
 And over the water to Charley.
 Charley loves good ale and wine,
And Charley loves good brandy,
And Charley loves a pretty girl,
As sweet as sugar-candy.

Over the water, and over the sea,
And over the water to Charley,
I'll have none of your nasty beef,
Nor I'll have none of your barley;
But I'll have some of your very best flour;
To make a white cake for my Charley.

Up Hill and down Dale.

UP hill and down dale;
 Butter is made in every vale;
 And if that Nancy Cook
Is a good girl,
She shall have a spouse,
And make butter anon,
Before her old grandmother
Grows a young man.

Elizabeth.

ELIZABETH, Eliza, Betsy, and Bess,
 Went over the water to rob a bird's nest,
 They found a nest with five eggs in it,
They each took one, and left four in it.

[111]

The Alphabet.

A was an angler,
  Went out in a fog;
Who fish'd all the day,
  And caught only a frog.

    B was cook Betty,
      A-baking a pie
    With ten or twelve apples
      All piled up on high.

        C was a custard
          In a glass dish,
        With as much cinnamon
          As you could wish.

D was fat Dick,
  Who did nothing but eat;
He would leave book and play
  For a nice bit of meat.

    E was an egg,
      In a basket with more,
    Which Peggy will sell
      For a shilling a score.

        F was a fox,
          So cunning and sly:
        Who looks at the hen-roost—
          I need not say why.

G was a greyhound,
  As fleet as the wind;
In the race or the course
  Left all others behind.

H was a heron,
  Who lived near a pond;
Of gobbling the fishes
  He was wondrously fond.

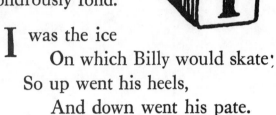

I was the ice
  On which Billy would skate;
So up went his heels,
  And down went his pate.

J was Joe Jenkins,
  Who played on the fiddle;
He began twenty tunes,
  But left off in the middle.

K was a kitten,
  Who jumped at a cork,
And learned to eat mice
  Without plate, knife, or fork.

L was a lark,
  Who sings us a song,
And wakes us betimes
  Lest we sleep too long.

M was Miss Molly,
  Who turned in her toes,
And hung down her head
  Till her knees touched her nose.

[113]

N was a nosegay,
Sprinkled with dew,
Pulled in the morning
And presented to you.

O was an owl,
Who looked wondrously wise;
But he's watching a mouse
With his large round eyes.

P was a parrot,
With feathers like gold,
Who talks just as much,
And no more than he's told.

Q is the Queen
Who governs the land,
And sits on a throne
Very lofty and grand.

R is a raven
Perched on an oak,
Who with a gruff voice
Cries croak, croak, croak!

S was a stork
With a very long bill,
Who swallows down fishes
And frogs to his fill.

T is a trumpeter
Blowing his horn,
Who tells us the news
As we rise in the morn.

U is a unicorn,
  Who, as it is said,
Wears an ivory bodkin
  On his forehead.

  V is a vulture
    Who eats a great deal,
  Devouring a dog
    Or a cat as a meal.

    W was a watchman
      Who guarded the street,
    Lest robbers or thieves
      The good people should meet.

X was King Xerxes,
  Who, if you don't know,
Reigned over Persia
  A great while ago.

  Y is the year
    That is passing away,
  And still growing shorter
    Every day.

    Z is a zebra,
      Whom you've heard of before;
    So here ends my rhyme
      Till I find you some more.

Master I have, and I am his Man.

MASTER I have, and I am his man,
    Gallop a dreary dun;
    Master I have, and I am his man,
And I'll get a wife as fast as I can;
With a heighty gaily gamberally,
    Higgledy piggledy, niggledy, niggledy,
    Gallop a dreary dun.

Little Bob Snooks.

LITTLE Bob Snooks was fond of his books,
    And loved by his usher and master:
    But naughty Jack Spry, he got a black eye,
And carries his nose in a plaster.

To Market, to Market.

TO market, to market,
    To buy a penny bun.
    Home again, home again,
Market is done.

On Christmas Eve I turned the Spit.

ON Christmas eve I turned the spit,
    I burnt my fingers, I feel it yet;
    The cock sparrow flew over the table,
The pot began to play with the ladle;
The ladle stood up like a naked man,
And vowed he'd fight the frying-pan;
The frying-pan behind the door
Said he never saw the like before;
And the kitchen clock I was going to wind,
Said he never saw the like behind.

[116]

"TO MARKET, TO MARKET, TO BUY A PENNY BUN"

Old Grimes.

OLD Grimes is dead, that good old man,
    You'll never see him more;
    He used to wear a long brown coat,
That buttoned down before.

Bow, wow, wow.

BOW, wow, wow,
    Whose dog art thou?
    Little Tom Tinker's dog,
Bow, wow, wow.

Ring around a Rosie.

RING around a rosie,
    A bottle full of posie,
    All the girls in our town,
Ring for little Josie.

Oh, dear, what can the Matter be?

OH, dear, what can the matter be?
    Two old women got up in an apple-tree;
    One came down,
And the other stayed till Saturday.

———

THERE was a girl in our towne,
    Silk an' satin was her gowne,
    Silk an' satin, gold an' velvet,
Guess her name—three times I've tell'd it.

(Ann.)

Jenny was a pretty Girl.

JENNY was a pretty girl,
But Fanny was a better;
Jenny looked like any churl,
When little Fanny let her.

Jenny had a pretty nose,
But Fanny had a better;
Jenny oft would come to blows,
But Fanny would not let her.

Jenny had a pretty doll,
But Fanny had a better;
Jenny chatted like a poll,
When little Fanny let her.

Jenny had a pretty son,
But Fanny had a better;
Jenny would sing all day long,
But Fanny would not let her.

Punch and Judy.

PUNCH and Judy
Fought for a pie,
Punch gave Judy
A knock in the eye.

Says Punch to Judy,
"Will you have any more?"
Says Judy to Punch,
"My eyes are too sore."

Three Men in a Tub.

HEY, rub-a-dub-dub, three men in a tub,
And who do you think were there?
The butcher, the baker, the candlestick maker,
And all had come from the fair.

Pussy-Cat ate the Dumplings.

PUSSY-CAT ate the dumplings, the dumplings,
    Pussy-cat ate the dumplings
    Mamma stood by, and cried, "Oh, fie!
Why did you eat the dumplings?"

Old Father Grey Beard.

OLD father Grey Beard,
    Without tooth or tongue;
    If you'll give me your finger,
I'll give you my thumb.

When I was a little Girl.

WHEN I was a little girl, about seven years old,
    I hadn't got a petticoat to cover me from the cold;
    So I went into Darlington, that pretty little town,
And there I bought a petticoat, a cloak, and a gown,
I went into the woods and built me a kirk,
And all the birds of the air, they helped me to work.
The hawk, with his long claws, pulled down the stone,
The dove, with her rough bill, brought me them home:
The parrot was the clergyman, the peacock was the clerk,
The bullfinch played the organ, and we made merry work.

Hey, my Kitten, my Kitten.

HEY, my kitten, my kitten,
   And hey, my kitten, my deary!
   Such a sweet pet as this
Was neither far nor neary.
Here we go up, up, up,
And here we go down, down, downy;
And here we go backwards and forwards,
And here we go round, round, roundy.

There was a jolly Miller.

THERE was a jolly miller
   Lived on the river Dee:
   He worked and sang from morn till night,
No lark so blithe as he,
And this the burden of his song
   Forever used to be—
"I jump mejerrime jee!
   I care for nobody—no! not I,
Since nobody cares for me."

A Pie sate on a Pear-Tree.

A PIE sate on a pear-tree,
   A pie sate on a pear-tree,
   A pie sate on a pear-tree,
Heigh O, heigh O, heigh O!
Once so merrily hopped she,
Twice so merrily hopped she,
Thrice so merrily hopped she,
Heigh O, heigh O, heigh O!

Little Betty Blue.

LITTLE Betty Blue
Lost her holiday shoe.
What shall little Betty do?
Buy her another
To match the other,
And then she'll walk in two.

A Swarm of Bees.

A SWARM of bees in May
Is worth a load of hay;
A swarm of bees in June
Is worth a silver spoon;
A swarm of bees in July
Is not worth a fly.

Cross Patch.

CROSS patch, draw the latch;
Sit by the fire and spin;
Take a cup and drink it up,
Then call your neighbors in.

That's all.

THERE was an old man,
And he had a calf,
And that's half;
He took him out of the stall,
And put him on the wall;
And that's all.

[122]

Ten little Children.

TEN little Children standing in a line—
One went home, and then there were nine.

Nine little Children swinging on a gate—
One tumbled off, and then there were eight.

Eight little Children never heard of heaven—
One kicked the bucket, and then there were seven.

Seven little Children cutting up tricks—
One went to bed and then there were six.

Six little Children kicking all alive—
One broke his neck, and then there were five.

Five little Children on a cellar door—
One tumbled off, and then there were four.

Four little Children climbing up a tree—
One fell down, and then there were three.

Three little Children out in a canoe—
One fell overboard, and then there were two.

Two little Children fooling with a gun—
One shot the other, and then there was one.

One little Child was living all alone—
He got married, and then there was none.

Goosey, Goosey, Gander.

GOOSEY, goosey, gander,
 Where dost thou wander?
 Up stairs and down stairs,
And in my lady's chamber.
There I met an old man
Who would not say his prayers,
I took him by the hind legs
And threw him down stairs.

Fa, la, la, la, lal, de.

THERE were two birds sat on a stone,
 Fa, la, la, la, lal, de;
 One flew away and then there was one,
Fa, la, la, la, lal, de;
The other flew after, and then there was none,
 Fa, la, la, la, lal, de;
And so the poor stone was left all alone,
 Fa, la, la, la, lal, de!

Of these two birds one back again flew,
 Fa, la, la, la, lal, de;
The other came after, and then there were two,
 Fa, la, la, la, lal, de;
Said one to the other,
  "Pray how do you do?"
 Fa, la, la, la, lal, de;
"Very well, thank you, and pray how do you?"
 Fa, la, la, la, lal, de!

[124]

"GOOSEY, GOOSEY, GANDER, WHERE DOST THOU WANDER?"

Christmas Days.

THE first day of Christmas,
My true love sent to me
A partridge in a pear-tree.

The second day of Christmas,
My true love sent to me
Two turtle-doves, and
A partridge in a pear-tree.

The third day of Christmas,
My true love sent to me
Three French hens,
Two turtle-doves, and
A partridge in a pear-tree.

The fourth day of Christmas,
My true love sent to me
Four colly birds,
Three French hens,
Two turtle-doves, and
A partridge in a pear-tree.

The fifth day of Christmas,
My true love sent to me
Five gold rings,
Four colly birds,
Three French hens,
Two turtle-doves, and
A partridge in a pear-tree.

The sixth day of Christmas,
My true love sent to me
Six geese a-laying,
Five gold rings,
Four colly birds,
Three French hens,
Two turtle-doves, and
A partridge in a pear-tree.

The seventh day of Christmas,
My true love sent to me
Seven swans a-swimming,
Six geese a-laying,
Five gold rings,
Four colly birds,
Three French hens,
Two turtle-doves, and
A partridge in a pear-tree.

The eighth day of Christmas,
My true love sent to me
Eight maids a-milking,
Seven swans a-swimming,
Six geese a-laying,
Five gold rings,
Four colly birds,
Three French hens,
Two turtle-doves, and
A partridge in a pear-tree.

The ninth day of Christmas,
My true love sent to me
Nine drummers drumming,
Eight maids a-milking,
Seven swans a-swimming,
Six geese a-laying,
Five gold rings,
Four colly birds,
Three French hens,
Two turtle-doves, and
A partridge in a pear-tree.

The tenth day of Christmas,
My true love sent to me
Ten pipers piping,
Nine drummers drumming,
Eight maids a-milking,
Seven swans a-swimming,
Six geese a-laying,
Five gold rings,
Four colly birds,
Three French hens,
Two turtle-doves, and
A partridge in a pear-tree.

The eleventh day of Christmas,
My true love sent to me
Eleven ladies dancing,
Ten pipers piping,
Nine drummers drumming,
Eight maids a-milking,
Seven swans a-swimming,
Six geese a-laying,
Five gold rings,
Four colly birds,
Three French hens,
Two turtle-doves, and
A partridge in a pear-tree.

The twelfth day of Christmas,
My true love sent to me
Twelve lords a-leaping,
Eleven ladies dancing,
Ten pipers piping,
Nine drummers drumming,
Eight maids a-milking,
Seven swans a-swimming,
Six geese a-laying,
Five gold rings,
Four colly birds,
Three French hens,
Two turtle-doves, and
A partridge in a pear-tree.

Blow, Wind, blow! and go, Mill, go!

BLOW, wind, blow!
and go, mill, go!
   That the miller may grind his corn;
That the baker may take it,
And into rolls make it,
And send us some hot in the morn.

Old Rhyme on cutting Nails.

CUT them on Monday, you cut them for health;
   Cut them on Tuesday, you cut them for wealth;
   Cut them on Wednesday, you cut them for news;
Cut them on Thursday, a pair of new shoes;
Cut them on Friday, you cut them for sorrow;
Cut them on Saturday, you'll see your true-love to-morrow;
Cut them on Sunday, and you'll have ill-fortune all through the
   week.

How do you do, Neighbour?

HOW do you do, neighbour?
   Neighbour, how do you do?
   Very well, I thank you.
How does Cousin Sue do?
She is very well,
And sends her love unto you,
And so does Cousin Bell.
Ah! how, pray, does she do?

[129]

Little Girl, little Girl.

LITTLE girl, little girl, where have you been?
Gathering roses to give to the Queen.
Little girl, little girl, what gave she you?
She gave me a diamond as big as my shoe.

Ding, dong, Bell.

DING, dong, bell,
The cat's in the well.
Who put her in?
Little Johnny Green.
Who pulled her out?
Great Johnny Stout.
What a naughty boy was that
To drown poor pussy cat,
Which never did him any harm,
But killed the mice in his father's barn.

There was a Little Man and he woo'd a Little Maid.

THERE was a little man,
And he wooed a little maid,
And he said, "Little maid, will you wed, wed, wed?
I have little more to say,
Than will you, yea or nay,
For least said is soonest mended-ded, ded, ded."
The little maid replied,
Some say a little sighed,
"But what shall we have for to eat, eat, eat?
Will the love that you're so rich in
Make a fire in the kitchen?
Or the little god of Love turn the spit, spit, spit?"

[130]

"DING, DONG, BELL, THE CAT'S IN THE WELL"

Yet didn't you see.

YET didn't you see, yet didn't you see,
    What naughty tricks they put upon me:
    They broke my pitcher
    And spilt my water,
    And huffed my mother,
    And chid her daughter,
    And kissed my sister instead of me.

Pat-a-cake, pat-a-cake.

PAT-A-CAKE, pat-a-cake, baker's man!
    Make me a cake, as fast as you can:
    Pat it, and prick it, and mark it with T,
Put it in the oven for Tommy and me.

There was a mad Man.

THERE was a mad man,
    And he had a mad wife,
    And they lived all in a mad lane.
They had three children all at a birth,
And they too were mad every one.
The father was mad,
The mother was mad,
The children all mad beside;
And upon a mad horse they all of them got,
And madly away did ride.

[132]

Could ye?

I WOULD if I could,
   If I couldn't how could I?
   I couldn't, without I could, could I?
Could you, without you could, could ye?
Could ye, could ye?
Could you, without you could, could ye?

When good King Arthur ruled this Land.

WHEN good King Arthur ruled this land,
   He was a goodly king;
   He stole three pecks of barley-meal,
To make a bag-pudding.

'A bag-pudding the king did make,
   And stuff'd it well with plums:
And in it put great lumps of fat,
   As big as my two thumbs.

The king and queen did eat thereof,
   And noblemen beside;
And what they could not eat that night,
   The queen next morning fried.

Is John Smith within?

IS John Smith within?
   Yes, that he is.
   Can he set a shoe?
Ay, marry, two.
Here a nail, there a nail,
Now your horse is shoed.

"Oh, what have you got for Dinner?"

"OH, what have you got for dinner, Mrs. Bond?"
  "There's beef in the larder, and ducks in the pond.
  Dilly, dilly, ducklings, come and be killed,
For you must be stuffed, and my customers filled!

"John Ostler, go fetch me a duckling or two,
John Ostler, go fetch me a duckling or two;
Cry dilly, dilly, ducklings, come and be killed,
For you must be stuffed, and my customers filled!"

"I have been to the ducks that are swimming in the pond,
And they won't come to be killed, Mrs. Bond;
I cried dilly, dilly, ducklings, come and be killed,
For you must be stuffed, and the customers filled!"

Mrs. Bond she went down to the pond in a rage,
With plenty of onions, and plenty of sage;
She cried, "Come, little wag-tails, come and be killed,
For you shall be stuffed, and my customers filled!"

Dame Trot and her Cat.

DAME TROT and her cat
    Sat down for to chat,
    The Dame sat on this side,
And Puss sat on that.
"Puss," says the Dame,
"Can you catch a rat,
Or a mouse in the dark?"
"Purr," says the cat.

[134]

Once I saw a little Bird.

ONCE I saw a little bird
   Come hop, hop, hop;
   So I cried, "Little bird,
Will you stop, stop, stop?"
And was going to the window
   To say "How do you do?"
But he shook his little tail,
   And away he flew.

Here comes a poor Widow from Babylon.

HERE comes a poor widow from Babylon,
   With six poor children all alone,
   One can bake, and one can brew,
One can shape, and one can sew,
One can bake a cake for the king.
Come choose you east, come choose you west,
Come choose you the one that you love best.

[135]

There was a jovial Beggar.

THERE was a jovial beggar,
    He had a wooden leg,
    Lame from his cradle,
And forced for to beg.
And a-begging we will go, we'll go, we'll go;
And a-begging we will go!

    A bag for his oatmeal,
        Another for his salt;
    And a pair of crutches,
        To show that he can halt.
    And a-begging we will go, we'll go, we'll go;
    And a-begging we will go!

    A bag for his wheat,
        Another for his rye;
    A little bottle by his side
        To drink when he's a-dry.
    And a-begging we will go, we'll go, we'll go;
    And a-begging we will go!

        Seven years I begged
            For my old Master Wild,
        He taught me to beg
            When I was but a child.
        And a-begging we will go, we'll go, we'll go;
        And a-begging we will go!

I begged for my master,
    And got him store of pelf;
And now, Jove be praised!
    I'm begging for myself.
And a-begging we will go, we'll go, we'll go;
And a-begging we will go!

In a hollow tree
    I live, and pay no rent;
Providence provides for me,
    And I am well content.
And a-begging we will go, we'll go, we'll go;
And a-begging we will go!

Of all the occupations,
    A beggar's life's the best;
For whene'er he's weary,
    He'll lay him down and rest.
And a-begging we will go, we'll go, we'll go;
And a-begging we will go!

I fear no plots against me,
    I live in open cell;
Then who would be a king,
    When beggars live so well?
And a-begging we will go, we'll go, we'll go;
And a-begging we will go!

Come, let's to Bed.

COME, let's to bed,
    Says Sleepy-head;
    Tarry a while, says Slow.
Put on the pan,
Says Greedy Nan,
Let's sup before we go.

I had a little Castle.

I HAD a little castle upon the sea-shore,
    One half was water, the other was land;
    I opened the castle door, and guess what I found,
I found a fair lady with a cup in her hand.
The cup was all gold, filled with wine,
"Drink, fair lady, and thou shalt be mine."

Dance, little Baby.

DANCE, little baby, dance up high,
    Never mind, baby, mother is by;
    Crow and caper, caper and crow,
There, little baby, there you go;
Up to the ceiling, down to the ground,
Backwards and forwards, round and round;
Dance, little baby, and mother will sing,
With the merry coral, ding, ding, ding!

[138]

"COME, LET'S TO BED, SAYS SLEEPY-HEAD"

When I was a little Boy.

WHEN I was a little boy,
   I washed my mammy's dishes,
   I put my finger in my eye,
And pulled out golden fishes.

Thomas A Tattamus.

THOMAS A TATTAMUS took two T's,
   To tie two tups to two tall trees,
   To frighten the terrible Thomas A Tattamus!
Tell me how many T's there are in *THAT.*

There was an old Woman sold Puddings and Pies.

THERE was an old woman
   Sold puddings and pies;
   She went to the mill,
And the dust flew in her eyes.
Now through the streets,
To all she meets,
She ever cries,
"Hot pies—Hot pies!"

Hush thee, my Babby.

HUSH thee, my babby,
   Lie still with thy daddy,
   Thy mammy has gone to the mill
To grind thee some wheat,
To make thee some meat,
And so, my dear babby, lie still.

[140]

The old Woman of Exeter.

THERE dwelt an old woman at Exeter;
When visitors came it sore vexed her,
So for fear they should eat,
She locked up all her meat,
This stingy old woman of Exeter.

Old Mother Twitchett.

OLD Mother Twitchett had but one eye,
And a long tail which she let fly;
And every time she went through a gap
A bit of her tail she left in the trap.

(A needle.)

There was an old Crow.

THERE was an old crow
Sat upon a clod;
There's an end of my song
That's very odd!

Upon St. Paul's Steeple.

UPON St. Paul's steeple stands a tree,
As full of apples as may be,
The little boys of London town,
They run with hooks and pull them down;
And then they run from hedge to hedge
Until they come to London Bridge.

[141]

January brings the Snow.

JANUARY brings the snow,
　　Makes our feet and fingers glow.

February brings the rain,
Thaws the frozen lake again.

March brings breezes loud and shrill,
Stirs the dancing daffodil.

April brings the primrose sweet,
Scatters daisies at our feet.

May brings flocks of pretty lambs,
Skipping by their fleecy dams.

June brings tulips, lilies, roses,
Fills the children's hands with posies.

Hot July brings cooling showers,
Apricots and gillyflowers.

August brings the sheaves of corn,
Then the harvest home is borne.

Warm September brings the fruit,
Sportsmen then begin to shoot.

Fresh October brings the pheasant,
Then to gather nuts is pleasant.

Dull November brings the blast,
Then the leaves are whirling fast.

Chill December brings the sleet,
Blazing fire and Christmas treat.

A was an Archer.

A was an archer, and shot at a frog,
B was a butcher, and had a great dog.
C was a captain, all covered with lace,
D was a drunkard, and had a red face.
E was an esquire, with pride on his brow,
F was a farmer, and followed the plough.
G was a gamester, who had but ill luck,
H was a hunter, and hunted a buck.
I was an innkeeper, who loved to bouse,
J was a joiner, and built up a house.
K was King William, once governed this land,
L was a lady, who had a white hand.
M was a miser, and hoarded up gold,
N was a nobleman, gallant and bold.
O was an oyster wench, and went about town,
P was a parson, and wore a black gown.
Q was a queen, who was fond of good flip,
R was a robber, and wanted a whip.
S was a sailor, and spent all he got,
T was a tinker, and mended a pot.
U was an usurer, a miserable elf,
V was a vintner, who drank all himself.
W was a watchman, and guarded the door,
X was expensive, and so became poor.
Y was a youth, that did not love school,
Z was a zany, a poor harmless fool.

[143]

I had a little Husband.

I HAD a little husband
  No bigger than my thumb,
I put him in a pint pot,
  And there I bid him drum.

  I bought a little horse,
    That galloped up and down;
  I bridled him, and saddled him,
    And sent him out of town.

    I gave him some garters,
      To garter up his hose,
    And a little handkerchief,
      To wipe his pretty nose.

There was an old Man of Tobago.

THERE was an old man of Tobago,
  Who lived on rice, gruel, and sago;
    Till, much to his bliss,
    His physician said this—
"To a leg, sir, of mutton you may go."

See, saw, Margery Daw.

SEE, saw, Margery Daw,
  Jenny shall have a new master;
  She shall have but a penny a day,
  Because she can't work any faster.

Ride, Baby, ride.

RIDE, baby, ride,
　　Pretty baby shall ride,
　　And have a little puppy-dog tied to her side,
And little pussy-cat tied to the other,
And away she shall ride to see her grandmother,
　　To see her grandmother,
　　To see her grandmother.

Cherries are ripe.

CHERRIES are ripe, cherries are ripe,
　　Give the baby some;
　　Cherries are ripe, cherries are ripe,
Baby must have none.

Cherries are too sour to use,
Babies are too young to choose;
By-and-by, baked in a pie,
Baby shall have some.

Rosy, and Colin, and Dun.

THERE was an old woman had three cows,
　　Rosy, and Colin, and Dun;
　　Rosy and Colin were sold at the fair,
And Dun broke his head in a fit of despair:
And there was an end of her three cows,
　　Rosy, and Colin, and Dun.

Rain, Rain, go to Spain.

RAIN, rain, go to Spain,
　　And never come back again.

[145]

Little Polly Flinders.

LITTLE Polly Flinders
Sat among the cinders,
Warming her pretty little toes!
Her mother came and caught her,
And whipped her little daughter,
For spoiling her nice new clothes.

If all the Seas were one Sea.

IF all the seas were one sea,
What a *great* sea that would be!
And if all the trees were one tree,
What a *great* tree that would be!
And if all the axes were one axe,
What a *great* axe that would be!
And if all the men were one man,
What a *great* man that would be!
And if the *great* man took the *great* axe,
And cut down the *great* tree,
And let it fall into the *great* sea,
What a splish-splash *that* would be!

If you Sneeze on Monday.

IF you sneeze on Monday, you sneeze for danger;
Sneeze on a Tuesday, kiss a stranger;
Sneeze on a Wednesday, sneeze for a letter;
Sneeze on a Thursday, something better;
Sneeze on a Friday, sneeze for sorrow;
Sneeze on a Saturday, see your sweetheart to-morrow.

"LITTLE POLLY FLINDERS SAT AMONG THE CINDERS"

Little Jack Jelf.

LITTLE Jack Jelf
  Was put on the shelf
  Because he could not spell "pie";
When his aunt, Mrs. Grace,
Saw his sorrowful face,
She could not help saying, "Oh, fie!"

  And since Master Jelf
  Was put on the shelf
Because he could not spell "pie,"
  Let him stand there so grim,
  And no more about him,
For I wish him a very good-bye!

Dance a Baby diddy.

DANCE a baby diddy,
  What can a mother do wid'e
  But sit in a lap,
And give him some pap,
Dance a baby diddy.

Hush-a-Bye, Baby.

HUSH-A-BYE, baby,
  Daddy is near;
  Mamma is a lady,
And that's very clear.

———

Christmas comes but once a year,
And when it comes it brings good cheer.

[148]

Diddle-y-diddle-y-dumpty.

DIDDLE-y-diddle-y-dumpty,
    The cat run up the plum-tree,
    Half-a-crown
To fetch her down,
Diddle-y-diddle-y-dumpty.

I will sing you a Song.

I WILL sing you a song,
    Though 'tis not very long,
    Of the woodcock and the sparrow,
Of the little dog that burned his tail,
And he shall be whipped to-morrow.

Tit, tat, toe.

TIT, tat, toe,
    My first go,
    Three jolly butcher boys
All of a row;
Stick one up,
Stick one down,
Stick one in the old man's crown.

———

If "ifs" and "ands"
Were pots and pans,
There would be no need for tinkers!

[149]

A Frog he would a-wooing go.

A FROG he would a-wooing go,
   Heigho, says Rowley,
Whether his mother would let him or no,
With a rowley powley, gammon and spinach,
Heigho, says Anthony Rowley!

So off he set with his opera hat,
      Heigho, says Rowley,
And on the road he met with a rat.
      With a rowley powley, gammon and spinach,
      Heigho, says Anthony Rowley!

"Pray, Mr. Rat, will you go with me,"
      Heigho, says Rowley,
"Kind Mrs. Mousey for to see?"
   With a rowley powley, gammon and spinach,
   Heigho, says Anthony Rowley!

When they reached the door of Mousey's hall,
      Heigho, says Rowley,
They gave a loud knock, and they gave a loud call.
   With a rowley powley, gammon and spinach,
   Heigho, says Anthony Rowley!

"Pray, Mrs. Mouse, are you within?"
      Heigho, says Rowley,
"Oh, yes, kind sirs, I'm sitting to spin."
   With a rowley powley, gammon and spinach,
   Heigho, says Anthony Rowley!

[150]

"A FROG HE WOULD A-WOOING GO"

"Pray, Mrs. Mouse, will you give us some beer?"
Heigho, says Rowley,
"For Froggy and I are fond of good cheer."
With a rowley powley, gammon and spinach,
Heigho, says Anthony Rowley!

"Pray, Mr. Frog, will you give us a song?"
Heigho, says Rowley,
"But let it be something that's not very long."
With a rowley powley, gammon and spinach,
Heigho, says Anthony Rowley!

"Indeed, Mrs. Mouse," replied Mr. Frog,
Heigho, says Rowley,
"A cold has made me as hoarse as a hog."
With a rowley powley, gammon and spinach,
Heigho, says Anthony Rowley!

"Since you have caught cold, Mr. Frog," Mousey said,
Heigho, says Rowley,
"I'll sing you a song that I have just made."
With a rowley powley, gammon and spinach,
Heigho, says Anthony Rowley!

But while they were all a merry-making,
Heigho, says Rowley,
A cat and her kittens came tumbling in.
With a rowley powley, gammon and spinach,
Heigho, says Anthony Rowley!

The cat she seized the rat by the crown;
            Heigho, says Rowley,
The kittens they pulled the little mouse down.
    With a rowley powley, gammon and spinach,
        Heigho, says Anthony Rowley!

            This put Mr. Frog in a terrible fright;
                    Heigho, says Rowley,
            He put up his hat, and he wished them good-night.
                With a rowley powley, gammon and spinach,
                    Heigho, says Anthony Rowley!

                But as Froggy was crossing over a brook,
                        Heigho, says Rowley,
                A lily-white duck came and gobbled him up.
                    With a rowley powley, gammon and spinach,
                        Heigho, says Anthony Rowley!

So there was an end of one, two, and three,
            Heigho, says Rowley,
The Rat, the Mouse, and the little Froggee!
    With a rowley powley, gammon and spinach,
        Heigho, says Anthony Rowley!

As I was going by Charing Cross.

AS I was going by Charing Cross,
    I saw a black man upon a black horse;
        They told me it was King Charles the First;
Oh, dear! my heart was ready to burst.

Simple Simon met a Pieman.

SIMPLE SIMON met a pieman
  Going to the fair;
  Says Simple Simon to the pieman,
"Let me taste your ware."

      Says the pieman to Simple Simon,
        "Show me first your penny."
      Says Simple Simon to the pieman,
        "Indeed, I have not any."

          Simple Simon went a-fishing,
            For to catch a whale:
          All the water he had got
            Was in his mother's pail.

Here a little Child I stand.

HERE a little child I stand,
  Heaving up my either hand;
  Cold as paddocks though they be,
Here I lift them up to Thee,
For a benison to fall
On our meat and on us all!

Wash me and comb me.

WASH me and comb me,
  And lay me down softly,
  And lay me on a bank to dry,
That I may look pretty
When somebody comes by.
[154]

Three blind Mice.

THREE blind mice, see how they run!
They all ran after the farmer's wife,
Who cut off their tails with a carving-knife,
Did you ever see such a thing in your life?
As three blind mice.

Byran O'Lin.

BRYAN O'LIN and his wife and wife's mother,
They all went over a bridge together:
The bridge was broken, and they all fell in,
"Mischief take all!" quoth Bryan O'Lin.

As I walked by myself.

AS I walked by myself,
I talked to myself,
And the self-same self said to me,
Look out for thyself,
Take care of thyself,
For nobody cares for thee.
I answered myself,
And said to myself
In the self-same repartee,
Look to thyself,
Or not look to thyself,
The self-same thing will be.

[155]

The Dove and the Wren.

THE dove says coo, coo, what shall I do?
I can scarce maintain two.
Pooh, pooh! says the wren, I have got ten,
And keep them all like gentlemen!

Diddle, diddle Dumpling.

DIDDLE diddle dumpling, my son John,
Went to bed with his breeches on,
One stocking off, and one stocking on;
Diddle diddle dumpling, my son John.

Eggs, Butter, Cheese, Bread.

EGGS, butter, cheese, bread,
Stick, stock, stone, dead.
Stick him up, stick him down,
Stick him in the old man's crown.

March winds and April showers
Bring forth May flowers.

[156]

Gushy Cow bonny.

GUSHY cow bonny,
  Let down thy milk,
  And I will give thee a gown of silk;
A gown of silk and a silver tee,
If thou wilt let down thy milk to me.

Let us go to the Woods.

LET us go to the woods," says Richard to Robin,
  "Let us go to the woods," says Robin to Bobbin,
  "Let us go to the woods," says John all alone,
"Let us go to the woods," says every one.

"What to do there?" says Richard to Robin,
"What to do there?" says Robin to Bobbin,
"What to do there?" says John all alone,
"What to do there?" says every one.

"We will shoot a wren," says Richard to Robin,
"We will shoot a wren," says Robin to Bobbin,
"We will shoot a wren," says John all alone,
"We will shoot a wren," says every one.

"Then pounce, pounce," says Richard to Robin,
"Then pounce, pounce," says Robin to Bobbin,
"Then pounce, pounce," says John all alone,
"Then pounce, pounce," says every one.

"She is dead, she is dead," says Richard to Robin,
"She is dead, she is dead," says Robin to Bobbin,
"She is dead, she is dead," says John all alone.
"She is dead, she is dead," says every one.

"How shall we get her home?" says Richard to Robin,
"How shall we get her home?" says Robin to Bobbin,
"How shall we get her home?" says John all alone,
"How shall we get her home?" says every one.

"In a cart with six horses," says Richard to Robin,
"In a cart with six horses," says Robin to Bobbin,
"In a cart with six horses," says John all alone,
"In a cart with six horses," says every one.

"How shall we get her dressed?" says Richard to Robin,
"How shall we get her dressed?" says Robin to Bobbin,
"How shall we get her dressed?" says John all alone,
"How shall we get her dressed?" says every one.

"We will hire seven cooks," says Richard to Robin,
"We will hire seven cooks," says Robin to Bobbin,
"We will hire seven cooks," says John all alone,
"We will hire seven cooks," says every one.

Bat, Bat.

BAT, bat,
   Come under my hat,
      And I'll give you a slice of bacon;
   And when I bake,
      I'll give you a cake,
If I am not mistaken.

[158]

"BAT, BAT, COME UNDER MY HAT"

Apple-Pie Alphabet.

A was an apple-pie;
B bit it;
C cut it;
D dealt it;
E eat it;
F fought for it;
G got it;
H had it;
J joined it;
K kept it;
L longed for it;
M mourned for it;
N nodded at it;
O opened it;
P peeped in it;
Q quartered it;
R ran for it;
S stole it;
T took it;
V viewed it;
W wanted it;
X Y and Z all wished a piece of it.

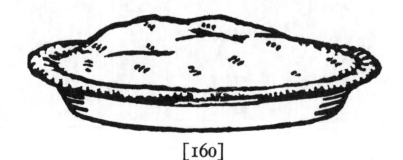

Doctor Faustus was a good Man.

DOCTOR FAUSTUS was a good man,
 He whipped his scholars now and then;
 When he whipped them he made them dance,

  Out of Scotland into France,
  Out of France into Spain,
  And then he whipped them back again!

One misty, moisty Morning.

ONE misty moisty morning,
 When cloudy was the weather,
 I chanced to meet an old man
Clothed all in leather.

He began to compliment,
And I began to grin;
How do you do, and how do you do?
And how do you do again?

Hickory, dickory, dock.

HICKORY, dickory, dock;
 The mouse ran up the clock;
 The clock struck one,
The mouse ran down,
Hickory, dickory, dock.

Doodle doodle doo.

DOODLE doodle doo,
   The Princess lost her shoe;
   Her Highness hopped,—
The fiddler stopped,
Not knowing what to do.

There was a little Boy went into a Barn.

THERE was a little boy went into a barn,
   And lay down on some hay;
   An owl came out and flew about,
And the little boy ran away.

The Cuckoo.

THE cuckoo's a fine bird,
   He sings as he flies;
   He brings us good tidings.
He tells us no lies.

He sucks little birds' eggs,
   To make his voice clear;
And when he sings "cuckoo!"
   The summer is near.

ALL of a row,
   Bend the bow,
   Shot at a pigeon,
And killed a crow.

[162]

In a Cottage in Fife.

IN a cottage in Fife
  Lived a man and his wife,
  Who, believe me, were comical folk;
  For to people's surprise,
  They both saw with their eyes,
And their tongues moved whenever they spoke!

  When quite fast asleep,
  I've been told that, to keep
Their eyes open they scarce could contrive:
  They walked on their feet,
  And 'twas thought what they eat
Helped, with drinking, to keep them alive!

Poor old Robinson Crusoe.

POOR old Robinson Crusoe!
  Poor old Robinson Crusoe!
  They made him a coat
Of an old nanny goat,
  I wonder how they could do so!
With a ring a ting tang,
And a ring a ting tang,
  Poor old Robinson Crusoe!

Humpty Dumpty.

HUMPTY DUMPTY sat on a wall,
  Humpty Dumpty had a great fall,
  Threescore men and threescore more
Cannot place Humpty Dumpty as he was before.

[163]

Gay go up.

GAY go up and gay go down,
    To ring the bells of London town.

Bull's eyes and targets,
Say the bells of St. Marg'ret's.

Brickbats and tiles,
Say the bells of St. Giles'.

Halfpence and farthings,
Say the bells of St. Martin's.

Oranges and lemons,
Say the bells of St. Clement's.

Pancakes and fritters,
Say the bells of St. Peter's.

Two sticks and an apple,
Say the bells at Whitechapel.

Old Father Baldpate,
Say the slow bells at Aldgate.

You owe me ten shillings,
Say the bells at St. Helen's.

Pokers and tongs,
Say the bells at St. John's.

Kettles and pans,
Say the bells at St. Ann's.

When will you pay me?
Say the bells at Old Bailey.

When I grow rich,
Say the bells at Shoreditch.

Pray when will that be?
Say the bells of Stepney.

I am sure I don't know,
Says the great bell at Bow.

Jenny Wren fell sick.

JENNY WREN fell sick,
    Upon a merry time;
    In came Robin Redbreast
    And brought her sops and wine.

"Eat well of the sop, Jenny,
    Drink well of the wine."
"Thank you, Robin, kindly,
    You shall be mine."

Jenny she got well,
    And stood upon her feet,
And told Robin plainly
    She loved him not a bit.

Robin being angry,
    Hopped upon a twig,
Saying, "Out upon you! Fie upon you,
    Bold-faced jig!"

[165]

Sukey, you shall be my Wife.

SUKEY, you shall be my wife,
 And I will tell you why:
  I have got a little pig,
 And you have got a sty;
I have got a dun cow,
 And you can make good cheese,
Sukey, will you have me?
 Say yes, if you please."

 Sukey she made answer,
  "For your cow and pig,
 I tell you, Jacky Jingle,
  I do not care a fig.

"I have got a puppy-dog,
 And a pussy-cat,
And I have got another thing
 That's better far than that.

  "For I have got a velvet purse
   That holds a hundred pound,
  'Twas left me by my grand-dad
   Who now lies underground.

  "So if your cow and pig
   Is all you have in store,
  You may go home and mind 'em,
   For now your wooing's o'er."

Says Jacky, "You're too hasty,
    I've got a horse and cart;
And I have got a better thing,—
    I've got a constant heart.

"If that won't do, then you may lay
    Your money on the shelf,
I soon shall get another girl
    That's better than yourself."

Then says little Sue,
"If your heart is true,
This trouble we'll get through,
    If things are rightly carried."
There's nothing more to do,
'Twixt Jacky and his Sue;
"None so happy as us two,
    For now we'll both be married!"

Now after they were married
    Some good things to produce,
Sukey's purse and hundred pounds
    Were quickly put in use;
Sukey milked the cow,
    And to make good cheese did try,
Jack drove his horse and cart,
    And minded pig and sty.

Little Tommy Tittlemouse.

LITTLE Tommy Tittlemouse
Lived in a little house;
He caught fishes
In other men's ditches.

The House that Jack built.

THIS is the house that Jack built.
This is the malt
That lay in the house that Jack built.

This is the rat,
That ate the malt
That lay in the house that Jack built.

This is the cat,
That killed the rat
That ate the malt
That lay in the house that Jack built.

This is the dog,
That worried the cat,
That killed the rat,
That ate the malt
That lay in the house that Jack built.

This is the cow with the crumpled horn,
That tossed the dog,
That worried the cat,
That killed the rat,
That ate the malt
That lay in the house that Jack built.

[168]

"LITTLE TOMMY TITTLEMOUSE, LIVED IN A LITTLE HOUSE"

This is the maiden all forlorn,
That milked the cow with the crumpled horn,
That tossed the dog,
That worried the cat,
That killed the rat,
That ate the malt
That lay in the house that Jack built.

This is the man all tattered and torn,
That kissed the maiden all forlorn,
That milked the cow with the crumpled horn,
That tossed the dog,
That worried the cat,
That killed the rat,
That ate the malt
That lay in the house that Jack built.

This is the priest all shaven and shorn,
That married the man all tattered and torn,
That kissed the maiden all forlorn,
That milked the cow with the crumpled horn,
That tossed the dog,
That worried the cat,
That killed the rat,
That ate the malt
That lay in the house that Jack built.

This is the cock that crowed in the morn,
That waked the priest all shaven and shorn,
That married the man all tattered and torn
That kissed the maiden all forlorn,
That milked the cow with the crumpled horn
That tossed the dog,
That worried the cat,
That killed the rat,
That ate the malt
That lay in the house that Jack built.

This is the farmer sowing his corn,
That kept the cock that crowed in the morn,
That waked the priest all shaven and shorn,
That married the man all tattered and torn.
That kissed the maiden all forlorn,
That milked the cow with the crumpled horn,
That tossed the dog,
That worried the cat,
That killed the rat,
That ate the malt
That lay in the house that Jack built.

As I was going o'er Westminster Bridge.

AS I was going o'er Westminster Bridge,
    I met with a Westminster scholar;
    He pulled off his cap, *an' drew* off his glove,
And wished me a very good-morrow.
    What is his name?

As I was a-going by a little Pig-sty.

AS I was going by a little pig-sty,
    I saw a child's petticoat hanging to dry,
    I took off my jacket and hung it hard by,
To bear the petticoat company.
The wind blew high, and down they fell;
Jacket and petticoat into the well.
Into the well, into the well,
Jacket and petticoat into the well.

Five Toes.

1.   "Let us go to the wood," says this pig;
2.   "What to do there?" says that pig;
3.   "To look for mother," says this pig;
4.   "What to do with her?" says that pig;
5.   "To kiss her, to kiss her," says this pig.

Where have you been all the Day?

"WHERE have you been all the day,
  My boy Tammy?"
"I've been all the day,
Courting of a lady gay:
But oh! she's too young
To be taken from her mammy."

  "What work can she do,
    My boy Tammy?
Can she bake and can she brew,
    My boy Tammy?"

"She can brew and she can bake,
And she can make our wedding cake:
But oh! she's too young
To be taken from her mammy."

"What age may she be?
What age may she be?
  My boy Tammy?"

"Twice two, twice seven,
Twice ten, twice eleven:
But oh! she's too young
To be taken from her mammy."

High, diddle doubt, my Candle's out.

HIGH, diddle doubt, my candle's out,
  My little maid is not at home;
Saddle my hog and bridle my dog,
And fetch my little maid home.

[173]

Rain, Rain, go away.

RAIN, rain, go away;
Come again another day;
Little Johnny wants to play.

This is the Death of Little Jenny Wren.

THIS is the death of
Little Jenny Wren,
And what the doctors
All said then.

Doctor Hawk felt her pulse,
And, shaking his head,
Said, "I fear I can't save her,
Because she's quite dead."

Doctor Hawk's a clever fellow,
He pinched her wrist enough to kill her.

"She'll do very well yet,"
Then said Doctor Fox,
"If she takes but one pill
From out of this box."

Jenny Wren was sick again,
And Jenny Wren did die;
The doctors vowed they'd cure her,
Or know the reason why.

[174]

Dame, get up and bake your Pies.

DAME, get up and bake your pies,
  Bake your pies, bake your pies;
  Dame, get up and bake your pies
On Christmas Day in the morning.

Dame, what makes your maidens lie,
  Maidens lie, maidens lie?
Dame, what makes your maidens lie
  On Christmas Day in the morning?

Dame, what makes your ducks to die,
  Ducks to die, ducks to die?
Dame, what makes your ducks to die
  On Christmas Day in the morning?

Their wings are cut and they cannot fly,
  Cannot fly, cannot fly,
Their wings are cut and they cannot fly
  On Christmas Day in the morning.

Birds of a Feather flock together.

BIRDS of a feather flock together,
  And so will pigs and swine;
  Rats and mice will have their choice,
And so will I have mine.

Go to Bed.

GO to bed first, a golden purse;
  Go to bed second, a golden pheasant;
  Go to bed third, a golden bird.
  [175]

A jolly old Sow.

A JOLLY old sow once lived in a sty,
  And three little piggies had she,
  And she waddled about saying "Grumph! grumph!
grumph!"
  While the little ones said "Wee! wee!"
And she waddled about saying "Grumph! grumph! grumph!"
  While the little ones said "Wee! wee!"

"My dear little piggies," said one of the brats,
  "My dear little brothers," said he,
"Let us all for the future say 'Grumph! grumph! grumph!'
  'Tis so childish to say 'Wee! wee!'
Let us all for the future say 'Grumph! grumph! grumph!'
  'Tis so childish to say 'Wee! wee!' "

These three little piggies grew skinny and lean,
  And lean they might very well be,
For somehow they couldn't say "Grumph! grumph! grumph!"
  And they wouldn't once say "Wee! wee!"
For somehow they couldn't say "Grumph! grumph! grumph!"
  And they wouldn't once say "Wee! wee!"

So after a time these little pigs died,
  They all died of fe-lo-de-see,
From trying too hard to say "Grumph! grumph! grumph!"
  When they only could say "Wee! wee!"
From trying too hard to say "Grumph! grumph! grumph!"
  When they only could say "Wee! wee!"

[176]

A moral there is to this little song,
A moral that's easy to see,
Don't try when you're young to say "Grumph! grumph!
grumph!"
When you only can say "Wee! wee!"
Don't try when you're young to say "Grumph! grumph!
grumph!"
When you only can say "Wee! wee!"

There was a Lady loved a Swine.

THERE was a lady loved a swine,
Honey, quoth she,
Pig-hog, wilt thou be mine?
Grunt, quoth he.

I'll build thee a silver stye,
Honey, quoth she;
And in it thou shalt lie;
Grunt, quoth he.

Pinned with a silver pin,
Honey, quoth she,
That you may go out and in;
Grunt, quoth he.

Wilt thou now have me,
Honey, quoth she;
Grunt, grunt, grunt, quoth he,
And went his way.

At the Siege of Belleisle.

AT the siege of Belleisle,
I was there all the while,
All the while, all the while,
At the siege of Belleisle.

V and I.

WHEN V and I together meet,
They make the number Six complete.
When I with V doth meet once more,
Then 'tis they Two can make but Four.
And when that V from I is gone
Alas! poor I can make but One.

Here we go up, up, up.

HERE we go up, up, up,
And here we go down, down, down,
And here we go backward and forward,
And here we go round, round, round.

Toss up my Darling.

TOSS up my darling, toss him up high,
Don't let his head, though, hit the blue sky.

[178]

Snail, Snail.

SNAIL, Snail, come out of your hole,
  Or else I'll beat you as black as a coal.
  Snail, Snail, put out your horns,
Here comes a thief to pull down your walls.

A Nick and a Nock.

A NICK and a nock,
    A hen and cock,
    And a penny for my master.

Little Robin Redbreast.

LITTLE Robin Redbreast
  Sat upon a rail:
  Niddle naddle went his head,
Wiggle waggle went his tail.

Cry, Baby, cry.

CRY, baby, cry,
  Put your finger in your eye,
  And tell your mother it wasn't I.

Bless you, Burny-Bee.

BLESS you, bless you, burny-bee:
    Say, when will your wedding be?
    If it be to-morrow day,
  Take your wings and fly away.

[179]

When I was a Bachelor.

WHEN I was a bachelor I lived by myself,
    And all the meat I got I put upon a shelf,
    The rats and the mice did lead me such a life,
That I went to London, to get myself a wife.

The streets were so broad, and the lanes were so narrow,
I could not get my wife home without a wheelbarrow,
The wheelbarrow broke, my wife got a fall,
Down tumbled wheelbarrow, little wife, and all.

Handy-Spandy.

HANDY-SPANDY, Jack-a-dandy,
    Loves plum-cake and sugar-candy.
    He bought some at a grocer's shop,
And pleased, away he went, hop, hop, hop.

There was a little Boy.

THERE was a little boy and a little girl
    Lived in an alley;
    Says the little boy to the little girl,
"Shall I, oh! shall I?"

                    Says the little girl to the little boy,
                        "What shall we do?"
                    Says the little boy to the little girl,
                        "I will kiss you."

"WHEN I WAS A BACHELOR I LIVED BY MYSELF"

As I went through the Garden Gap.

AS I went through the garden gap,
Who should I meet but Dick Redcap!
A stick in his hand, a stone in his throat:
If you'll tell me this riddle, I'll give you a groat.
(*A cherry.*)

Charley Warley.

CHARLEY WARLEY had a cow,
Black and white about the brow;
Open the gate and let her go through,
Charley Warley's old cow!

Now what do you think?

NOW what do you think
Of little Jack Jingle?
Before he was married
He used to live single.

Jack Sprat's Pig.

JACK SPRAT'S pig,
He was not very little,
Nor yet very big;
He was not very lean,
He was not very fat;
He'll do well for a grunt,
Says little Jack Sprat.

When a Twister a twisting.

WHEN a Twister a twisting, will twist him a twist;
    For the twisting of his twist, he three times doth intwist;
    But if one of the twines of the twist do untwist,
The twine that untwisteth, untwisteth the twist.

Untwirling the twine that untwisteth between,
He twirls, with the twister, the two in a twine:
Then twice having twisted the twines of the twine,
He twisteth the twine he had twined in twain.

The twain that, in twining, before in the twine,
As twines were intwisted; he now doth untwine:
'Twixt the twain inter-twisting a twine more between,
He, twirling his twister, makes a twist of the twine.

My little old Man and I fell out.

MY little old man and I fell out,
    I'll tell you what 'twas all about:
    I had money, and he had none,
And that's the way the row begun.

There once were two Cats.

THERE once were two cats of Kilkenny,
    Each thought there was one cat too many,
    So they fought and they fit,
And they scratched and they bit,
Till, excepting their nails
And the tips of their tails,
Instead of two cats, there weren't any.

There was an old Woman.

THERE was an old woman who rode on a broom,
  With a high gee ho, gee humble;
  And she took her old cat behind for a groom,
With a bimble, bamble, bumble.

They travelled along till they came to the sky,
  With a high gee ho, gee humble;
But the journey so long made them very hungry,
  With a bimble, bamble, bumble.

Says Tom, "I can find nothing here to eat,
  With a high gee ho, gee humble;
So let us go back again, I entreat,
  With a bimble, bamble, bumble."

The old woman would not go back so soon,
  With a high gee ho, gee humble;
For she wanted to visit the Man in the Moon,
  With a bimble, bamble, bumble.

Says Tom, "I'll go back by myself to our house,
  With a high gee ho, gee humble;
For there I can catch a good rat or a mouse,
  With a bimble, bamble, bumble."

"But," says the old woman, "how will you go?
  With a high gee ho, gee humble;
You shan't have my nag, I protest and vow,
  With a bimble, bamble, bumble."

[184]

"No, no," says Tom, "I've a plan of my own,"
  With a high gee ho, gee humble;
So he slid down the rainbow, and left her alone,
  With a bimble, bamble, bumble.

So now, if you happen to visit the sky,
  With a high gee ho, gee humble;
And want to come back, you Tom's method may try,
  With a bimble, bamble, bumble.

Robin Hood.

ROBIN HOOD, Robin Hood,
  Is in the mickle wood!
Little John, Little John,
He to the town is gone.
Robin Hood, Robin Hood,
  Is telling his beads,
All in the greenwood,
  Among the green weeds.
Little John, Little John,
  If he comes no more,
Robin Hood, Robin Hood,
  We shall fret full sore!

Yankee Doodle.

YANKEE DOODLE went to town,
  Upon a little pony;
  He stuck a feather in his hat,
And called it Macaroni.

[185]

Two little Kittens.

TWO little kittens, one stormy night,
  Began to quarrel and then to fight;
  One had a mouse, and the other had none,
And that's the way the quarrel begun.

"I'll have that mouse," said the biggest cat.
"*You'll* have that mouse? We'll see about that!"
"I *will* have that mouse," said the eldest son.
"You *sha'n't* have the mouse," said the little one.

I told you before 'twas a stormy night
When these two little kittens began to fight;
The old woman seized her sweeping broom,
And swept the two kittens right out of the room.

The ground was covered with frost and snow,
And the two little kittens had nowhere to go;
So they laid them down on the mat at the door,
While the old woman finished sweeping the floor.

Then they crept in, as quiet as mice,
All wet with the snow, and as cold as ice,
For they found it was better, that stormy night,
To lie down and sleep than to quarrel and fight.

Needles and Pins.

NEEDLES and pins, needles and pins,
  When a man marries his trouble begins.
[186]

I had a little Doggie.

I HAD a little doggie that used to sit and beg,
  But Doggie tumbled down the stairs, and broke his little leg.

Oh! Doggie, I will nurse you, and try to make you well;
And you shall have a collar with a pretty little bell.

Ah! Doggie, don't you think you should very faithful be,
For having such a loving friend to comfort you as me?

And when your leg is better, and you can run and play,
We'll have a scamper in the fields and see them making hay.

Cuckoo, Cuckoo,

CUCKOO, Cuckoo,
    What do you do?
      "In April
    I open my bill;
      In May
    I sing night and day;
      In June
    I change my tune;
      In July
    Away I fly;
      In August
    Away I must."

A Man went a-hunting at Reigate.

A MAN went a-hunting at Reigate,
    And wished to leap over a high gate.
    Says the owner, "Go round,
With your dog and your hound,
For you never shall leap over my gate."

[187]

I have seen you, little Mouse.

I HAVE seen you, little mouse,
　　Running all about the house,
　　Through the hole, your little eye
In the wainscot peeping sly,
Hoping soon some crumbs to steal,
To make quite a hearty meal.
Look before you venture out,
See if pussy is about,
If she's gone, you'll quickly run,
To the larder for some fun,
Round about the dishes creep,
Taking into each a peep,
To choose the daintiest that's there,
Spoiling things you do not care.

How many Miles?

HOW many miles is it to Babylon?—
　　Threescore miles and ten.
　　Can I get there by candle-light?—
Yes, and back again!
If your heels are nimble and light,
You may get there by candle-light.

Charley, Charley.

CHARLEY, Charley, stole the barley
　　Out of the baker's shop;
　　The baker came out, and gave him a clout,
And made poor Charley hop.

[188]

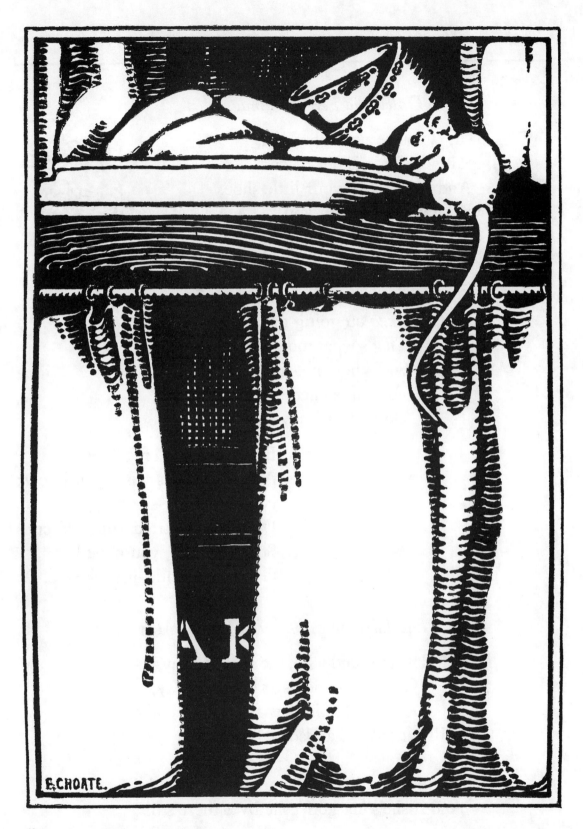

"I HAVE SEEN YOU LITTLE MOUSE"

Dolly and her Mamma.

DOLLY, you're a naughty girl,
　　All your hair is out of curl,
　　And you've torn your little shoe.
Oh! what must I do with you!
You shall only have dry bread;
Dolly, you shall go to bed.

　　Do you hear all that I say?
　　Are you going to obey?
　　That's what mother says to me,
　　So I know it's right, you see;
　　For I'm sometimes naughty too,
　　Dolly dear, as well as you.

　　　　But I mean to try to grow
　　　　All my parents wish, you know;
　　　　Never into passions fly,
　　　　Or when thwarted, sulk and cry.
　　　　So, my Dolly, you must be
　　　　Good and gentle, just like me.

The fair Maid who, the first of May.

THE fair maid who, the first of May,
　　Goes to the fields at break of day,
　　And washes in dew from the hawthorn tree,
Will ever after handsome be.

———

There was an old woman lived under a hill,
And if she's not gone, she lives there still.

Maggie's Pet.

SWEET Maggie had a little bird,
  And "Goldie" was his name,
  And on her hand he used to sit,
He was so very tame.
  Her rosy lips he'd often peck,
Which meant a loving kiss.
  Oh! would not you delight to have
A little bird like this?

A lump of sugar sweet and white,
Would Maggie give her Dick,
  And then she'd watch how eagerly
He'd fly to it and peck;
  And such a merry song he'd sing,
To thank her for the treat,
  For little birds, like little girls,
Like something nice to eat.

Mary had a pretty Bird.

MARY had a pretty bird,
  Feathers bright and yellow;
  Slender legs, upon my word,
He was a pretty fellow.
The sweetest notes he always sang,
  Which much delighted Mary;
And near the cage she'd ever sit,
  To hear her own canary.

[191]

I love Sixpence.

I LOVE sixpence, pretty little sixpence,
　I love sixpence better than my life;
　I spent a penny of it, I spent another,
And took fourpence home to my wife.

Oh, my little fourpence, pretty little fourpence,
　I love fourpence better than my life;
I spent a penny of it, I spent another,
　And I took twopence home to my wife.

Oh, my little twopence, my pretty little twopence,
　I love twopence better than my life;
I spent a penny of it, I spent another,
　And I took nothing home to my wife.

Oh, my little nothing, my pretty little nothing,
　What will nothing buy for my wife?
I have nothing, I spend nothing,
　I love nothing better than my wife.

Hector Protector.

HECTOR PROTECTOR was dressed all in green;
　Hector Protector was sent to the Queen.
　The Queen did not like him,
No more did the King:
So Hector Protector was sent back again.

The Toad and the Frog.

"CROAK!" said the Toad, "I'm hungry, I think,
To-day I've had nothing to eat or to drink;
I'll crawl to a garden and jump through the pales,
And there I'll dine nicely on slugs and on snails."
"Ho, ho!" quoth the Frog, "is that what you mean?
Then I'll hop away to the next meadow stream,
There I will drink, and eat worms and slugs too,
And then I shall have a good dinner like you."

———

RABBIT, Rabbit, Rabbit Pie!
Come, my ladies, come and buy;
Else your babies they will cry.

We are all in the Dumps.

WE are all in the dumps,
For diamonds are trumps,
The kittens are gone to St. Paul's;
The babies are bit,
The moon's in a fit,
And the houses are built without walls.

The Cock's on the Housetop.

THE cock's on the housetop blowing his horn;
The bull's in the barn a-threshing of corn;
The maids in the meadows are making of hay,
The ducks in the river are swimming away.

[193]

Three wise Men of Gotham.

THREE wise men of Gotham
Went to sea in a bowl.
If the bowl had been stronger,
My song had been longer.

Why is Pussy in Bed, pray?

WHY is pussy in bed, pray?
She is sick, says the fly,
And I fear she will die;
That's why she's in bed.

Pray, what's her disorder?
She's got a locked jaw,
Says the little jackdaw,
And that's her disorder.

Who makes her gruel?
I, says the horse,
For I am her nurse,
And I make her gruel.

Pray, who is her doctor?
Quack, quack! says the duck,
I that task undertook,
And I am her doctor.

Who thinks she'll recover?
I, says the deer,
For I did last year:
So I think she'll recover.

"THREE WISE MEN OF GOTHAM"

There was an old Woman of Leeds.

THERE was an old woman of Leeds
　　Who spent all her time in good deeds;
　　She worked for the poor
　Till her fingers were sore,
This pious old woman of Leeds!

I saw three Ships come sailing by.

I SAW three ships come sailing by,
　Sailing by, sailing by,
　I saw three ships come sailing by,
On New-Year's Day in the morning.

　And what do you think was in them then,
　　In them then, in them then?
　And what do you think was in them then,
　　On New-Year's Day in the morning?

　　Three pretty girls were in them then,
　　　In them then, in them then,
　　Three pretty girls were in them then,
　　　On New-Year's Day in the morning.

　　　And one could whistle, and one could sing,
　　　　And one could play on the violin,
　　　Such joy there was at my wedding,
　　　　On New-Year's Day in the morning.

Early to Bed.

EARLY to bed, and early to rise,
　Makes a man healthy, wealthy, and wise.

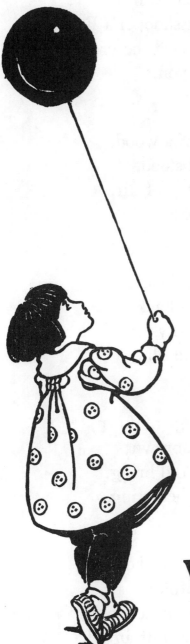

There was a little Girl.

THERE was a little girl
And she had a little curl,
Right in the middle of her forehead;
And when she was good,
She was very, very good—
But when she was bad she was horrid!

He loves me.

1. He loves me,
2.   He don't!
3. He'll have me,
4.   He won't!
5. He would if he could,
6. But he can't,
7.   So he don't!

———

SPEAK when you're spoken to,
Come when one call,
Shut the door after you,
And turn to the wall.

What is the News of the Day?

WHAT is the news of the day,
Good neighbour, I pray?
They say the balloon
Is gone up to the moon!

[197]

Come take up your Hats, and away let us haste.

COME take up your hats, and away let us haste,
   To the Butterfly's Ball, and the Grasshopper's Feast.
   The trumpeter, Gad-fly, has summoned the crew,
And the revels are now only waiting for you.

On the smooth shaven grass, by the side of a wood,
Beneath a broad oak which for ages had stood,
See the children of earth, and the tenants of air,
To an evening's amusement together repair.

And there came the Beetle so blind and so black,
Who carried the Emmet, his friend, on his back.
And there came the Gnat and the Dragon-fly too,
With all their relations, green, orange, and blue.

And there came the Moth, with her plumage of down,
And the Hornet with jacket of yellow and brown;
And with him the Wasp, his companion, did bring,
But they promised that evening to lay by their sting.

Then the sly little Dormouse peeped out of his hole,
And led to the Feast his blind cousin the Mole:
And the Snail, with her horns peeping out of her shell,
Came, fatigued with the distance, the length of an ell.

A mushroom the table, and on it was spread
A water-dock leaf, which their table-cloth made.
The viands were various, to each of their taste,
And the Bee brought the honey to sweeten the feast.

With steps most majestic the Snail did advance,
And he promised the gazers a minuet to dance;
But they all laughed so loud that he drew in his head,
And went in his own little chamber to bed.

Then, as evening gave way to the shadows of night,
Their watchman, the Glow-worm, came out with his light.
So home let us hasten, while yet we can see,
For no watchman is waiting for you or for me.

Jacky, come give me thy Fiddle.

JACKY, come give me thy fiddle,
    If ever thou mean to thrive.
    Nay; I'll not give my fiddle
    To any man alive.

If I should give my fiddle,
    They'll think that I'm gone mad;
For many a joyful day
    My fiddle and I have had.

Whistle, Daughter, whistle.

WHISTLE, daughter, whistle; whistle, daughter dear.
    I cannot whistle, mammy, I cannot whistle clear.
    Whistle, daughter, whistle, whistle for a pound.
I cannot whistle, mammy, I cannot make a sound.

Merry are the Bells.

MERRY are the bells, and merry would they ring,
Merry was myself, and merry could I sing;
With a merry ding-dong, happy, gay, and free,
And a merry sing-song, happy let us be!

Waddle goes your gait, and hollow are your hose,
Noddle goes your pate, and purple is your nose;
Merry is your sing-song, happy, gay, and free,
With a merry ding-dong, happy let us be!

Merry have we met, and merry have we been,
Merry let us part, and merry meet again;
With our merry sing-song, happy, gay, and free,
And a merry ding-dong, happy let us be!

The fat Man of Bombay.

THERE was a fat man of Bombay,
Who was smoking one sunshiny day,
When a bird, called a snipe,
Flew away with his pipe,
Which vexed the fat man of Bombay.

If I'd as much Money as I could spend.

IF I'd as much money as I could spend,
I never would cry old chairs to mend;
Old chairs to mend, old chairs to mend;
I never would cry old chairs to mend.
If I'd as much money as I could tell,
I never would cry old clothes to sell;
Old clothes to sell, old clothes to sell;
I never would cry old clothes to sell.

"THERE WAS A FAT MAN OF BOMBAY"

Come hither.

COME hither, little puppy dog;
  I'll give you a new collar,
  If you will learn to read your book
 And be a clever scholar.
No, no! replied the puppy dog,
  I've other fish to fry,
For I must learn to guard your house,
  And bark when thieves come nigh.
With a tingle, tangle, tit-mouse!
  Robin knows great A,
And B, and C, and D, and E, F, G, H, I, J, K.

Come hither, little pussy cat;
  If you'll your grammar study
I'll give you silver clogs to wear,
  Whene'er the gutter's muddy.
No! whilst I grammar learn, says Puss,
  Your house will in a trice
Be overrun from top to bottom
  With flocks of rats and mice.
With a tingle, tangle, tit-mouse!
  Robin knows great A,
And B, and C, and D, and E, F, G, H, I, J, K.

Come hither, pretty cockatoo;
  Come and learn your letters,
And you shall have a knife and fork
  To eat with, like your betters.
No, no! the cockatoo replied,

My beak will do as well;
I'd rather eat my victuals thus
   Than go and learn to spell.
With a tingle, tangle, tit-mouse!
   Robin knows great A,
And B, and C, and D, and E, F, G, H, I, J, K.

      Come hither, then, good little boy,
        And learn your alphabet,
      And you a pair of boots and spurs,
        Like your papa's, shall get.
      Oh, yes! I'll learn my alphabet;
        And when I well can read,
      Perhaps papa will give me, too,
        A pretty long-tail'd steed.
      With a tingle, tangle, tit-mouse!
        Robin knows great A,
      And B, and C, and D, and E, F, G, H, I, J, K.

There was a Man, and he had naught.

THERE was a man, and he had naught,
      And robbers came to rob him;
      He crept up to the chimney pot,
    And then they thought they had him.

    But he got down on t'other side,
      And then they could not find him;
    He ran fourteen miles in fifteen days,
      And never looked behind him.

Girls and Boys, come out to play.

GIRLS and boys, come out to play,
 The moon doth shine as bright as day.
  Leave your supper, and leave your sleep,
And meet your playfellows in the street,
Come with a whoop, come with a call,
Come with a good will or not at all.
Up the ladder and down the wall,
A halfpenny roll will serve us all;
You find milk, and I'll find flour,
And we'll have a pudding in half-an-hour.

A Duck and a Drake.

A DUCK and a drake,
  And a halfpenny cake,
   With a penny to pay the baker.
A hop and a scotch
Is another notch,
Slitherum, slatherum, take her.

As I was going along, long, long.

AS I was going along, long, long,
 A-singing a comical song, song, song,
  The lane that I went was so long, long, long,
And the song that I sung was as long, long, long,
And so I went singing along.

[204]

Tommy Trot, a Man of Law.

TOMMY TROT, a man of law,
Sold his bed and lay upon straw,—
Sold the straw and slept on grass,
To buy his wife a looking-glass.

The Child and the Star.

LITTLE star that shines so bright,
Come and peep at me to-night,
For I often watch for you
In the pretty sky so blue.

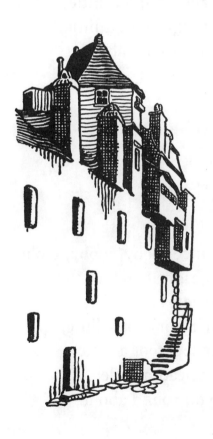

Little star! O tell me, pray,
Where you hide yourself all day?
Have you got a home like me,
And a father kind to see?

Little Child, at you I peep
While you lie so fast asleep;
But when morn begins to break,
I my homeward journey take.

For I've many friends on high,
Living with me in the sky;
And a loving Father, too,
Who commands what I'm to do.

[205]

Now we dance looby, looby, looby.

NOW we dance looby, looby, looby,
Now we dance looby, looby, light.
Shake your right hand a little,
And turn you round about.

Now we dance looby, looby, looby,
Shake your right hand a little,
Shake your left hand a little,
And turn you round about.

Now we dance looby, looby, looby,
Shake your right hand a little,
Shake your left hand a little,
Shake your right foot a little,
And turn you round about.

Now we dance looby, looby, looby,
Shake your right hand a little,
Shake your left hand a little,
Shake your right foot a little,
Shake your left foot a little,
And turn you round about.

Now we dance looby, looby, looby,
Shake your right hand a little,
Shake your left hand a little,
Shake your right foot a little,
Shake your left foot a little,
Shake your head a little,
And turn you round about.

[206]

Poor Dog Bright.

POOR Dog Bright
    Ran off with all his might,
    Because the cat was after him,
Poor Dog Bright.

Poor Cat Fright
Ran off with all her might,
Because the Dog was after her,
Poor Cat Fright.

Monday alone.

MONDAY alone,
    Tuesday together,
    Wednesday we walk
When it's fine weather.
Thursday we kiss,
Friday we cry,
Saturday's hours
Seem almost to fly.
But of all days in the week
We will call
Sunday, the rest day,
The best day of all.

Old Woman, old Woman.

OLD woman, old woman, shall we go a-shearing?
    Speak a little louder, sir,—I am very thick of hearing.
    Old woman, old woman, shall I love you dearly?
Thank you, kind sir. I hear you very clearly.

Three little Kittens.

THREE little kittens lost their mittens,
  And they began to cry,
    Oh! mother dear,
    We very much fear
That we have lost our mittens.

            Lost your mittens!
            You naughty kittens!
        Then you shall have no pie.
              Mee-ow, mee-ow, mee-ow.
        No, you shall have no pie.
              Mee-ow, mee-ow, mee-ow.

The three little kittens found their mittens,
  And they began to cry,
    Oh! mother dear,
    See here, see here!
See, we have found our mittens.

        Put on your mittens,
        You silly kittens,
      And you shall have some pie,
          Purr-r, purr-r, purr-r,
      Oh! let us have the pie!
          Purr-r purr-r, purr-r,

            The three little kittens put on their mittens,
            And soon ate up the pie;
              Oh! mother dear,
              We greatly fear,
          That we have soiled our mittens.
                    [208]

"THREE LITTLE KITTENS LOST THEIR MITTENS"

Soiled your mittens!
You naughty kittens!
Then they began to sigh,
 Mi-ow, mi-ow, mi-ow.
Then they began to sigh,
 Mi-ow, mi-ow, mi-ow.

 The three little kittens washed their mittens,
 And hung them up to dry;
 Oh! mother dear,
 Do you not hear,
 That we have washed our mittens?

 Washed your mittens!
 Oh! you're good kittens.
 But I smell a rat close by.
 Hush! hush! mee-ow, mee-ow.
 We smell a rat close by,
 Mee-ow, mee-ow, mee-ow.

One, He loves.

ONE, he loves; two, he loves;
 Three, he loves, they say;
 Four, he loves with all his heart;
Five, he casts away.
Six, he loves; seven, she loves;
Eight, they both love.
Nine, he comes; ten, he tarries;
Eleven, he courts; twelve, he marries.

Bessy Bell and Mary Gray.

BESSY BELL and Mary Gray,
    They were two bonny lasses:
    They built their house upon the lea,
And covered it with rashes.

Bessy kept the garden gate,
    And Mary kept the pantry:
Bessy always had to wait,
    While Mary lived in plenty.

When little Fred.

WHEN little Fred
    Was called to bed,
    He always acted right;
He kissed Mamma,
And then Papa,
And wished them all good-night.

He made no noise,
Like naughty boys,
But gently upstairs
Directly went,
When he was sent,
And always said his prayers.

The King of France, and the King of Spain.

THE King of France, with twenty thousand men,
    Went up the hill, and then came down again.
    The King of Spain, with twenty thousand more,
Climbed the same hill the French had climbed before.

[211]

The Fox and his Wife.

THE fox and his wife they had a great strife,
They never ate mustard in all their whole life;
They ate their meat without fork or knife,
And loved to be picking a bone, e-ho!

The fox jumped up on a moonlight night;
The stars they were shining, and all things bright;
Oh, ho! said the fox, it's a very fine night
For me to go through the town, e-ho!

The fox when he came to yonder stile,
He lifted his lugs and he listened awhile!
Oh, ho! said the fox, it's but a short mile
From this unto yonder wee town, e-ho!

The fox when he came to the farmer's gate,
Who should he see but the farmer's drake;
I love you well for your master's sake
And long to be picking your bone, e-ho!

The grey goose she ran round the haystack,
Oh, ho! said the fox, you are very fat;
You'll grease my beard and ride on my back
From this into yonder wee town, e-ho!

Old Gammer Hipple-hopple hopped out of bed,
She opened the casement, and popped out her head;
Oh! husband, oh! husband, the grey goose is dead,
And the fox is gone through the town, oh!

Then the old man got up in his red cap,
And swore he would catch the fox in a trap;
But the fox was too cunning, and gave him the slip,
   And ran through the town, the town, oh!

When he got to the top of the hill,
He blew his trumpet both loud and shrill,
For joy that he was safe through the town, oh!

When the fox came back to his den,
He had young ones both nine and ten,
"You're welcome home, daddy; you may go again,
If you bring us such nice meat
   From the town, oh!"

Johnny shall have a new Bonnet.

JOHNNY shall have a new bonnet,
   And Johnny shall go to the fair,
   And Johnny shall have a blue ribbon
   To tie up his bonny brown hair.
And why may not I love Johnny?
   And why may not Johnny love me?
And why may not I love Johnny
   As well as another body?
And here's a leg for a stocking,
   And here is a leg for a shoe,
And he has a kiss for his daddy,
   And two for his mammy, I trow.
And why may not I love Johnny?
   And why may not Johnny love me?
And why may not I love Johnny,
   As well as another body?

Polly, put the Kettle on.

POLLY, put the kettle on,
　　Polly, put the kettle on,
　　Polly, put the kettle on,
And we'll all have tea.

Sukey, take it off again,
　　Sukey, take it off again,
　　Sukey, take it off again,
　　They're all gone away.

Pit, pat, well-a-day.

PIT, pat, well-a-day,
　　Little Robin flew away;
　　Where can little Robin be?
But up in the cherry-tree.

———

Oh, the rusty, dusty, rusty miller!
I'll not change my wife for gold or siller.

———

UP hill spare me,
　　Down hill 'ware me,
　　On level ground spare me not,
And in the stable forget me not.

　　　　　　　　　　(A horse.)

[214]

"POLLY, PUT THE KETTLE ON"

Little Bo-Peep.

LITTLE Bo-Peep has lost her sheep,
    And can't tell where to find them;
    Leave them alone, and they'll come home,
Wagging their tails behind them.

Little Bo-Peep fell fast asleep,
And dreamt she heard them bleating;
When she awoke, 'twas a joke—
Ah! cruel vision so fleeting.

Then up she took her little crook,
Determined for to find them;
What was her joy to behold them nigh,
Wagging their tails behind them.

For want of a Nail.

FOR want of a nail, the shoe was lost,
    For want of the shoe, the horse was lost,
    For want of the horse, the rider was lost,
For want of the rider, the battle was lost,
For want of the battle, the kingdom was lost,
And all from the want of a horseshoe nail!

Jerry, James and John.

THERE was an old woman had three sons,
    Jerry and James and John:
    Jerry was hung, James was drowned,
John was lost, and never was found;
And there was an end of her three sons,
Jerry and James and John!

[216]

What is the Rhyme for Porringer?

WHAT is the rhyme for porringer?
The King he had a daughter fair,
And gave the Prince of Orange her.

The Way we ride.

TO market ride the gentlemen,
So do we, so do we;
Then comes the country clown;
Hobbledy gee, Hobbledy gee;
First go the ladies, nim, nim, nim;
Next come the gentlemen, trim, trim, trim;
Then come the country clowns, gallop-a-trot.

One-ery, two-ery.

ONE-ERY, two-ery,
Ziccary zan;
Hollow bone, crack a bone,
Ninery, ten;
Spittery spot,
It must be done;
Twiddleum twaddleum,
Twenty-one.

F FOR fig,
J for jig,
And N for knuckle-bones,
J for John the waterman,
And S for sack of stones.

[217]

Around the green Gravel.

AROUND the green gravel the grass grows green,
And all the pretty maids are plain to be seen;
Wash them with milk, and clothe them with silk,
And write their names with a pen and ink.

There was a little Woman.

THERE was a little woman, as I've been told,
Who was not very young, nor yet very old,
Now this little woman her living got,
By selling codlins, hot, hot, hot!

———

THE calf, the goose, the bee,
The world is ruled by these three.
(*Parchment, pens, and wax.*)

Jack Sprat had a Cat.

JACK SPRAT
Had a cat,
It had but one ear;
It went to buy butter,
When butter was dear.

If you are a Gentleman.

IF you are a gentleman, as I suppose you be,
You'll neither laugh nor smile at the tickling of your
knee.

The Hart he loves the high Wood.

THE Hart he loves the high wood,
The Hare she loves the hill,
The Knight he loves his bright sword,
The lady—loves her will.

I had a little Moppet.

I HAD a little moppet,
I kept it in my pocket,
And fed it with corn and hay,
There came a proud beggar
Who swore he would have her,
And stole little moppet away.

Robin and Richard.

ROBIN and Richard were two pretty men,
They lay in bed till the clock struck ten;
Then up starts Robin and looks in the sky;
"Oh, brother Richard, the sun's very high!
You go on with the bottle and bag,
And I'll come after with Jolly Jack Nag."

———

AWAKE, arise, pull out your eyes,
And hear what time of day;
And when you have done, pull out your tongue,
And see what you can say.

[219]

A little cock Sparrow.

A LITTLE cock sparrow sat on a green tree.
   And he cherupped, he cherupped, so merry was he.
   A little cock sparrow sat on a green tree,
And he cherupped, he cherupped, so merry was he.

   A naughty boy came with his wee bow and arrow,
   Determined to shoot this little cock sparrow,
   A naughty boy came with his wee bow and arrow,
   Determined to shoot this little cock sparrow.

   "This little cock sparrow shall make me a stew,
   And his giblets shall make me a little pie too."
   "Oh, no!" said the sparrow, "I *won't* make a stew."
   So he flapped his wings and away he flew!

Friday Night's Dream.

FRIDAY night's dream
   On the Saturday told,
   Is sure to come true,
Be it never so old.

Peter White.

PETER WHITE,
   Will ne'er go right.
   Would you know the reason why?
He follows his nose,
Wherever he goes,
And that stands all awry.

———

AS round as an apple, as deep as a cup,
   And all the king's horses can't pull it up.
                  (*A well.*)

"A LITTLE COCK SPARROW SAT ON A GREEN TREE"

Away, Birds, away!

AWAY, birds, away!
    Take a little, and leave a little,
    And do not come again;
For if you do,
I will shoot you through,
And then there will be an end of you.

With a Hop, Step, and a Jump.

THE miller he grinds his corn, his corn;
    The miller he grinds his corn, his corn;
    The little boy blue comes winding his horn,
      With a hop, step, and a jump.

The carter he whistles aside his team;
The carter he whistles aside his team;
And Dolly comes tripping with the nice clouted cream,
    With a hop, step, and a jump.

The nightingale sings when we're at rest;
The nightingale sings when we're at rest;
The little bird climbs the tree for his nest,
    With a hop, step, and a jump.

The damsels are churning for curds and whey;
The damsels are churning for curds and whey;
The lads in the field are making the hay,
    With a hop, step, and a jump.

To Market, to Market, to buy a fat Pig.

TO market, to market, to buy a fat pig,
    Home again, home again, jiggety jig.
    To market, to market, to buy a fat hog,
Home again, home again, jiggety jog.

Matthew, Mark, Luke, and John,

MATTHEW, Mark, Luke, and John,
    Bless the bed that I lie on.
    Four corners to my bed,
Four angels round my head,
One to sing, and one to pray,
And two to carry my soul away.

Lavender blue and Rosemary green.

LAVENDER blue and rosemary green,
    When I am king you shall be queen;
    Call up my maids at four o'clock,
Some to the wheel and some to the rock,
Some to make hay and some to shear corn,
And you and I will keep ourselves warm.

One, two, three, four.

ONE, two, three, four,
    Mary at the cottage door;
    Five, six, seven, eight,
Eating berries off a plate;
O-U-T spells out!

————

Long legs, crooked thighs,
Little head, and no eyes.

                (Pair of tongs.)

[223]

Little Jack Horner.

LITTLE Jack Horner sat in a corner
 Eating his Christmas pie.
 He put in his thumb and pulled out a plum
And said what a good boy am I.

Dance to your Daddy.

DANCE to your daddy,
 My little babby,
 Dance to your daddy,
My little lamb.

You shall have a fishy
In a little dishy;
You shall have a fishy
When the boat comes in.

The old Woman must stand at the Tub.

THE old woman must stand at the tub, tub, tub,
 The dirty clothes to rub, rub, rub;
 But when they are clean, and fit to be seen,
She'll dress like a lady, and dance on the green.

Little Drops of Water.

LITTLE drops of water,
 Little grains of sand,
 Make the mighty ocean,
And the wondrous land.

Pussy Cat Mole.

PUSSY Cat Mole,
   Jump'd over a coal,
   And in her best petticoat burnt a great hole.
Poor pussy's weeping, she'll have no more milk
Until her best petticoat's mended with silk.

Lend me thy Mare.

"LEND me thy mare to ride a mile?"
   "She is lamed, leaping over a stile."
   "Alack! and I must keep the fair!
I'll give thee money for thy mare."
"Oh, oh, say you so?
Money will make the mare to go!"

Come, my Children.

COME, my children, come away,
   For the sun shines bright to-day;
   Little children, come with me,
Birds and brooks and posies see;
Get your hats and come away,
For it is a pleasant day.

Everything is laughing, singing,
All the pretty flowers are springing;
See the kitten, full of fun,
Sporting in the brilliant sun;
Children too may sport and play,
For it is a pleasant day.

[225]

I like little Pussy.

I LIKE little pussy, her coat is so warm,—
  And if I don't hurt her she'll do me no harm;
  I'll not pull her tail, nor drive her away,
But pussy and I very gently will play.

There was an old Man.

THERE was an old man who lived in a wood,
  As you may plainly see;
  He said he could do as much work in a day
As his wife could do in three.

"With all my heart," the old woman said;
  "If that you will allow,
To-morrow you'll stay at home in my stead,
  And I'll go drive the plough;

    But you must milk the Tidy cow,
      For fear that she go dry;
    And you must feed the little pigs
      That are within the stye;

And you must mind the speckled hen,
  For fear she lay away;
And you must reel the spool of yarn
  That I span yesterday."

[226]

"I LIKE LITTLE PUSSY, HER COAT IS SO WARM"

A curious discourse.

A CURIOUS discourse about an Apple-pie, that passed between the Twenty-five Letters at Dinner-time.

Says A, Give me a good large slice.
Says B, A little Bit, but nice.
Says C, Cut me a piece of Crust.
Says D, It is as Dry as Dust.
Says E, I'll Eat now, fast who will.
Says F, I vow I'll have my Fill.
Says G, Give it to me Good and Great.
Says H, A little bit I Hate.
Says I, I love the Juice the best.
And K the very same confessed.
Says L, There's nothing more I Love.
Says M, it makes your teeth to Move.
N Noticed what the others said.
O Others' plates with grief surveyed.
P Praised the cook up to the life.
Q Quarreled 'cause he'd a bad knife.
Says R, It Runs short, I'm afraid.
S Silent sat, and nothing said.
T thought that Talking might lose time.
U Understood it at meals a crime.
W Wished there had been a quince in.
Says X, Those cooks there's no convincing.
Says Y, I'll eat, let others wish.
Z sat as mute as any fish.
While ampersand, he licked the dish.

I had a little Pony.

I HAD a little pony,
   They called him Dapple Grey,
   I lent him to a lady,
To ride a mile away.

   She whipped him, she lashed him,
   She drove him through the mire,
   I wadna gie my pony yet
   For all the lady's hire.

One, two, three, four, five.

ONE, two, three, four, five,
   I have caught a fish alive;
   Six, seven, eight, nine, ten,
I have let it go again.
Why did you let it go?
Because it bit my finger so.
Which finger did it bite?
The little one on the right.

A long-tailed Pig.

A LONG-TAILED pig, and a short-tailed pig,
   Or a pig without e'er a tail,
   A sow pig, or a boar pig,
Or a pig with a curly tail.

——

   See, see. What shall I see?
   A horse's head where his tail should be.
[229]

Oh, who is so merry.

OH, who is so merry, so merry, heigh ho!
   As the light-hearted fairy, heigh ho! heigh ho!
     He dances and sings
     To the sound of his wings,
With a hey and a heigh and a ho!

   Oh, who is so merry, so airy, heigh ho!
   As the light-hearted fairy, heigh ho! heigh ho!
     His nectar he sips
     From a primrose's lips,
   With a hey and a heigh and a ho!

     Oh, who is so merry, so merry, heigh ho!
     As the light-footed fairy, heigh ho! heigh ho!
       His night is the noon
       And his sun is the moon,
     With a hey and a heigh and a ho!

Oh dear, what can the matter be?

OH dear, what can the matter be?
   Johnny's so long at the fair,
   He promised to buy me a bunch of blue ribbons
To tie up my bonny brown hair.

Ring-a-ring-a Roses.

RING-a-ring-a roses,
   A pocket full of posies;
   Hush-hush-hush,
We'll all tumble down.

[230]

The art of good Driving.

THE art of good driving's a paradox quite.
　　Though custom has proved it so long;
　　If you go to the left, you are sure to go right,
If you go to the right, you go wrong.

The Cock doth crow.

THE cock doth crow
　　To let you know,
　　If you be wise
'Tis time to rise.

———

A sunshiny shower
Won't last half an hour.

In the Month of February.

IN the month of February,
　　When green leaves begin to spring,
　　Little lambs do skip like fairies,
Birds do couple, build, and sing.

Come when you're called.

COME when you're called,
　　Do what you're bid,
　　Shut the door after you,
Never be chid.

Jerry Hall, he is so small,
A rat could eat him, hat and all.

Georgey Porgey.

GEORGEY PORGEY, pudding and pie,
  Kissed the girls and made them cry;
  When the girls came out to play,
Georgey Porgey ran away.

Jack Jingle.

JACK JINGLE went 'prentice
    To make a horseshoe,
  He wasted the iron
    Till it would not do.
  His master came in,
    And began for to rail;
  Says Jack, "The shoe's spoiled,
    But 'twill still make a nail."

  He tried at the nail,
    But, chancing to miss,
  Says, "If it won't make a nail,
    It shall yet make a hiss."
  Then into the water
    Threw the hot iron, smack.
  "Hiss!" quoth the iron;
    "I thought so," says Jack.

Buttons a Farthing a pair.

BUTTONS a farthing a pair,
    Come, who will buy them of me?
    They're round and sound and pretty,
And fit for the girls of the city.
Come, who will buy them of me,
Buttons a farthing a pair?

"GEORGEY, PORGEY, PUDDING AND PIE"

Hushy Baby, my Doll.

HUSHY baby, my doll, I pray you don't cry,
    And I'll give you some bread and some milk by-and-by;
    Or, perhaps you like custard, or maybe a tart,—
Then to either you're welcome, with all my whole heart.

But how, my dear baby, shall I make you eat
Of the bread, or the milk, or the custard, or meat?
For those pretty red lips seem shut up so fast,
I much fear they won't open to taste the repast.

Ah! but then, my sweet child, you'll surely not cry,
Oh no, not one tear is there now in your eye;
Come kiss me, my dear, then, although you're but wood,
For I'm sure now you smile, and look very good.

Molly, my Sister, and I fell out.

MOLLY, my sister, and I fell out,
    And what do you think it was about?
    She loved coffee and I loved tea,
And that was the reason we couldn't agree.

———

BLACK we are, but much admired;
    Men seek for us till they are tired.
    We tire the horse, but comfort man;
Tell me this riddle if you can.
                                    (*Coal.*)

[234]

There were three jovial Welshmen.

THERE were three jovial Welshmen,
  As I have heard them say,
  And they would go a-hunting
Upon St. David's day.

          All the day they hunted,
            And nothing could they find;
          But a ship a-sailing,
            A-sailing with the wind.

One said it was a ship,
  The other he said "Nay;"
The third said it was a house,
  With the chimney blown away.

          And all the night they hunted,
            And nothing could they find,
          But the moon a-gliding,
            A-gliding with the wind.

                  One said it was the moon,
                    The other he said "Nay;"
                  The third said it was a cheese,
                    And half o' it cut away.

Margery Mutton-Pie.

MARGERY Mutton-pie and Johnny Bo-peep,
  They met together in Gracechurch-Street;
  In and out, in and out, over the way,
Oh! says Johnny, 'tis chop-nose day.

[235]

The old Woman and her Pig.

AN old woman was sweeping her house, and she found a little crooked sixpence.

"What," said she, "shall I do with this little sixpence? I will go to market, and buy a little pig."

As she was coming home, she came to a stile; but the pig would not go over the stile.

She went a little farther, and she met a dog. So she said to the dog—

"Dog, dog, bite pig!
Pig won't get over the stile;
And I shan't get home to-night."

But the dog would not.

She went a little farther, and she met a stick. So she said—

"Stick, stick, beat dog!
Dog won't bite pig;
Pig won't get over the stile;
And I shan't get home to-night."

But the stick would not.

She went a little farther, and she met a fire. So she said—

"Fire, fire, burn stick!
Stick won't beat dog;
Dog won't bite pig;
Pig won't get over the stile;
And I shan't get home to-night."

"THE OLD WOMAN AND HER PIG"

But the fire would not.

She went a little farther, and she met some water. So she said—

"Water, water, quench fire!
Fire won't burn stick;
Stick won't beat dog;
Dog won't bite pig;
Pig won't get over the stile;
And I shan't get home to-night."

But the water would not.

She went a little farther, and she met an ox. So she said—

"Ox, ox, drink water!
Water won't quench fire;
Fire won't burn stick;
Stick won't beat dog;
Dog won't bite pig;
Pig won't get over the stile;
And I shan't get home to-night."

But the ox would not.

She went a little farther, and she met a butcher. So she said—

"Butcher, butcher, kill ox!
Ox won't drink water;
Water won't quench fire;
Fire won't burn stick;
Stick won't beat dog;
Dog won't bite pig;
Pig won't get over the stile;
And I shan't get home to-night."

But the butcher would not.

She went a little farther, and she met a rope. So she said—

"Rope, rope, hang butcher!
Butcher won't kill ox;
Ox won't drink water;
Water won't quench fire;
Fire won't burn stick;
Stick won't beat dog;
Dog won't bite pig;
Pig won't get over the stile;
And I shan't get home to-night."

But the rope would not.

She went a little farther, and she met a rat. So she said—

"Rat, rat, gnaw rope!
Rope won't hang butcher;
Butcher won't kill ox;
Ox won't drink water;
Water won't quench fire;
Fire won't burn stick;
Stick won't beat dog;
Dog won't bite pig;
Pig won't get over the stile;
And I shan't get home to-night."

But the rat would not.

She went a little farther, and she met a cat. So she said—

"Cat, cat, kill rat!
Rat won't gnaw rope;
Rope won't hang butcher·
Butcher won't kill ox;
Ox won't drink water;
Water won't quench fire;
Fire won't burn stick;
Stick won't beat dog;
Dog won't bite pig;
Pig won't get over the stile;
And I shan't get home to-night."

The cat said, "If you will give me a saucer of milk, I will kill the rat."

So the old woman gave the cat the milk, and when she had lapped up the milk—

The cat began to kill the rat;
The rat began to gnaw the rope;
The rope began to hang the butcher;
The butcher began to kill the ox;
The ox began to drink the water;
The water began to quench the fire;
The fire began to burn the stick;
The stick began to beat the dog;
The dog began to bite the pig;
The pig jumped over the stile;
And so the old woman got home that night.